John Bowen

THE
DISORDERLY
WOMEN

LONDON
METHUEN & CO LTD
11 NEW FETTER LANE EC4

First published 1969 by Methuen & Co, Ltd.
© 1969 by John Bowen

Printed in Great Britain by
COX & WYMAN LTD,
LONDON AND READING

For the past, present and
future students of the
London Academy of Music
and Dramatic Art

FOREWORD

If myths are archetypical (as well as being symbolic accounts of what has actually occurred at times for which almost no other accounts have survived), then they must be relevant, for those societies which have remembered them, as long as they are remembered. Yet at particular times they may seem to have a particularly strong relevance, and it seems that now – April 1969, as I write – is such a time for the myth of the Bacchae. The same month as my own play, *The Disorderly Women*, opened at the Stables Theatre Club, Manchester, the National Theatre, in a programme of experimental plays at the Jeanetta Cochrane, mounted a one-act version by Maureen Duffy, set in a Ladies' Lavatory. The Methuen Playscripts series has an Australian version by Rodney Milgate. A kind of improvised entertainment (in which the audience were encouraged to enjoy the actors in a fuller sense than is usual in the theatre) called *Dionysus 1969* has been playing in New York, and it is not so long since Robert Bolt offered us in *Gentle Jack* his own statement of the myth. Since I greatly admire Mr Bolt's work, even though *Gentle Jack* seemed to me a failure, I used a record by the Manfred Mann Group called *My Name is Jack* to introduce both the acts of my own play. It was a very private joke, and nobody understood it.

Nevertheless, although the idea of an archetype presupposes a general relevance to the human condition, human beings are also particular people, and their ways of interpreting this generality will be different and individual. For the director and cast of *Dionysus 1969*, it seems that the myth of the Bacchae is an expression of joy, showing how sexual reticence and social conformity may be broken down and human beings find the truth about life and themselves in instinctive behaviour. Miss Duffy seems to use the myth as a feminist statement. I myself have presented it as a tragic story, in which a good man, attempting to perform good acts, is destroyed by what during

my schooldays used to be called 'the fatal flaw' in his own
nature, in this case by his refusal to accept the imperfectibility
of man, his denial both in himself and others of what is
instinctive, irrational, irresponsible, selfish and destructive.
I have attempted to make explicit what may be implicit in
Euripides' play, that the myth of the Bacchae is primarily
about the fight between Apollo and Dionysus, in which
Dionysus wins.

Put this to someone born after 1945, and he may tell you,
'Quite right. Dionysus ought to win. Instinctive behaviour is
what life is for.' My own designer at Manchester, Christopher
Hewitt, was in no doubt that the play was saying, 'Dionysus
good. Pentheus bad,' and produced an all-grey Thebes in
support of his belief. (Eventually we compromised between
his view of Thebes and mine by giving Pentheus a rose to
wear on the jacket of his costume, and putting something red
on each of the desks in the administrative offices.) But I was
born in 1924, and grew up in the nineteen-thirties. I am one
of those middle-aged liberals in this country, who voted Labour
until Hugh Gaitskell died, and have felt politically directionless
ever since. I used to believe that most crime was a by-product
of poverty, that the idea of social justice and the spread of an
education which would teach people to evaluate evidence so as
to make their own choices between opposing arguments would
cure most political and social ills. I believed that men did not
want to hurt each other, though they might be tricked into
doing so. When I was a child, E. Nesbit was my favourite
author, and by the end of a remarkably protracted adolescence,
Bloomsbury and Fabianism had come together to form my
beliefs. I believed as Pentheus does:

'We are more than animals . . . We have intelligence, forethought and memory. We perceive harmony, and respond
to logic. We have compassion and concern: we care for
each other. What must the law do, then, but help us to be
the difference between men and animals ? – to be most
truly ourselves. Such laws . . . are made by all men together, in free argument and persuasion. Those who break

the law must be punished, for they have broken the strength
of our city, but none may be punished who has not broken
the law.'

and again:

'PENTHEUS. We make a good life for our people here.
I tried to make you understand that. Nothing in excess.
Everything in moderation. Everything works. Everyone
has a part to play in the life of the city. Balance. Equality.
Freedom under the law. Respect. Even those who do the
dirtiest and most monotonous jobs have compensation and
respect.

DIONYSUS. A noble ideal!

PENTHEUS. Yes. A reasonable society. It's not exciting,
but it is noble.'

Well, it *is* noble, but the facts are against it. The facts of
Auschwitz, Dachau, Buchenwald, Dresden, Hiroshima, Naga-
saki, Vietnam are against it, more facts than we know of in the
U.S.S.R. and the Chinese People's Republic, more than we
know of in Africa, more everywhere. And crime, it seems, is
not much to do with poverty. In certain people the pre-
disposition to criminal behaviour is overwhelming, and it is
present in us all. Liberal democracy is only one of many
ineffective forms of government, and all over the world it is
giving way to various forms of dictatorship. Educational opportunity, at least in Britain and the U.S.A. is more widely spread
than ever before, and far from wishing to choose between
opposing arguments, many of the newly educated refuse even
to give a hearing to any argument opposed to their own beliefs,
and the reiterated bleating of 'Four Legs good! Two legs bad!'
is to be heard, not in *Animal Farm* but at most British universi-
ties. If my 1969 self were to return to 1945, it could only say,
'I have seen the future, and it doesn't work.'

The Disorderly Women, then, is a work of pessimism, which
may help to explain why there are so many jokes in it. At the
end, Pentheus is dead, his work undone, and it is clear that
Thebes will revert (under the Senior Departmental Secretary)
to the dictatorship it was in his father's time. 'Dionysus wins',

but of course 'winning' in social and political terms is meaningless to Dionysus: instinctive behaviour is not concerned with such terms. In a practical sense, Dionysus has 'won' as a child wins when it knocks down building-blocks: someone else has to build the blocks up again, and it doesn't much matter who does it. The victory is what matters: anyone may turn it to account. Pentheus has 'denied' Dionysus – that is, he has denied the strength of instinct both in others and himself, and in consequence 'his own flesh killed him'. Yet instinctive man is still man. Man is a social being, and needs to build social institutions. So over and over again, within each society and within each man, there occurs the Argument I have placed before Act Two of this play. If it were only a two-way argument between the desire to exercise power and the need in any social system for fairness, 'understanding, tolerance, rational thought', then it might be settled, and probably in favour of social justice, but whenever settlement seems likely, the third participant says, 'Your terms have no meaning for me, and I shall destroy the winner.'

I have suggested that much of this may be implicit in Euripides' play, but Euripides never wrote a foreword to the published text of *The Bacchae*, and there is some disagreement about the play's meaning. Mr. Philip Vellacott, in the excellent introduction to his translation of the play for Penguin Books, mentions 'two unsatisfactory theories'. The first is that Euripides, after a lifetime of scepticism, became converted to religious belief, and wrote *The Bacchae* to show what happens to disbelievers. The second is that the play is intended to show how people may be led into dreadful acts by a religious frenzy brought on by misinterpreting natural events as miracles.

But these are extreme views. Leave them aside, and there is still ambiguity. Whether Euripides intended, as Gilbert Murray suggested, to 'glorify' Dionysus, whether an old man, living in exile in Macedonia and bitter at the sophisticated Athenians who had driven him out, found a new delight in nature and was driven to express it in poetry, whether a famous playwright who had found refuge at the court of a rustic king thought it prudent to pick a subject that would please his patron (for the Dionysus cult entered Greece from the north east), whether nevertheless the end of the play expresses a revulsion from the cult or the conclusion that nature is terrible as well as delightful, whether all these and many whethers besides, it seems to me that the ambiguity in the play arises from Euripides' characterization of Pentheus, whom he presents as an obstinate, choleric and stupid tyrant, no kind of antagonist for a god. There is no 'tragic hero', no 'dramatic conflict', no 'fatal flaw', nothing of that sort. Instead there is, at the *explicit* level, a simple moral tale about a bad man who defies a god, and is most horribly punished. Like Shockheaded Peter and the boy who sucked his thumbs and had them cut off by the Scissors Man, he suffers a punishment altogether disproportionate to the offence. *We* may say that the dramatist deliberately chooses such a victim so that we may feel revulsion for the divine behaviour itself, uncoloured by any feelings of sympathy with the man, but we only have one line ('Gods should be free from human passions' – the passion for revenge in this case) to support us, and we must acknowledge the possibility of other opinions.

Ambiguous plays may be great plays, and *The Bacchae* is one of them, but I did not wish to write *The Bacchae* over again. I have been preoccupied with myth for much of my writing life, as anyone who is acquainted with my novel (and later play), *After The Rain*, and my novel, *A World Elsewhere*, will know: even my first novel, *The Truth Will Not Help Us*, long since remaindered, made an attempt to use history as myth. I wanted to do what Euripides did, what all the Greek dramatists did, what in our own century Giraudoux, Sartre and Anouilh have done, to go back to the myth and write the story in my own way. My Pentheus is very different from Euripides' Pentheus; Tiresias does not appear in my play; Cadmus is no longer the king's grandfather, but has become an old tutor, raised to head the administration of the city when the young king succeeds his father.

Yet anyone can tell that at certain points there are close correspondences between *The Bacchae* and my play. The Policeman's story in Act One is clearly a version of the

Herdsman's speech; some of the Messenger's speech has been given to my Junior Departmental Secretary; Dionysus' speech to the audience at the end of Act One is said to the Bacchae in *The Bacchae*; the Argument Before Act Two, though it expresses three conflicting points of view, has largely been lifted from one of the great choruses. And from the moment that Agave returns, carrying her son's head, *The Bacchae* and *The Disorderly Women* come very close together.

The reason is simple, and not admirable. I carry the wish to write a particular play or novel around with me for a long time, and if at the end of that time (for *A World Elsewhere*, ten years) the wish is still alive, I start to write. When I thought I was ready to write *The Disorderly Women*, I suggested to Norman Ayrton, the Principal of L.A.M.D.A., that I might direct third-year students in a first draft to try it out, and he cheerfully agreed. I began to read seriously. I read all the translations of *The Bacchae* I could find, and Professor Dodds' commentary, and R. P. Winnington-Ingram's *Euripides and Dionysus*, and various general works – Robert Graves' *Greek Myths* inevitably among them – for the myth itself, and I read up on the effect of the hallucinatory drugs, and talked to people who had tried marihuana and L.S.D., and then I started to write.

Meanwhile *Little Boxes* had opened at the Hampstead Theatre Club, and against our expectations transferred to the Duchess Theatre, and for various reasons I found myself far more involved in the mechanics of the transfer and the run than a playwright usually is, and suddenly the day when I must start rehearsals at L.A.M.D.A. was close, and my first draft was nowhere near written.

I took two kinds of remedial action. One was, from my own point of view, entirely successful. The two scenes in Act Two which we called 'Down Memory Lane' and 'Revival Meeting' were the result of a day spent with Agave and the six women, lying in the sun on the roof of the L.A.M.D.A. Theatre, talking, improvising, trying to find out why each woman had decided to drop out. The second action was more desperate, and its benefits were mixed. I patched the other holes in my own draft with pieces of loosely adapted Euripides.

Then I discovered an unexpected disadvantage in this trial run. Sure enough, it taught me what didn't work, and I was able to rewrite all that before the play's first professional production in Manchester. But it also taught me what did work, and I found myself unable to rewrite something which had worked well in performance, simply for the sake of taking it further away from Euripides. I needed a set speech from the Policeman at that point in the play; I needed it to arouse exactly the emotions it did arouse; I needed something which was violent and 'uncivilized', and which also demanded bravura acting to shock both Pentheus and the audience. I was stuck (you should excuse the *jeu de mots*) with some of my patches.

Well, there they are, and if their presence should lead some people to believe that *The Disorderly Women* is no more than a free adaptation of *The Bacchae*, that is the consequence of my own act. But it may be useful for those who wish to read, or act, or attend a performance of my own play, if I mention some of the ways in which the myth itself has led me on from Euripides' treatment of it.

First, the mushrooms. Robert Graves, both in his foreword to the 1960 edition of *The Greek Myths* (Penguin) and at much greater length in an essay, *What Food the Centaurs Ate*, published in *Steps* (Cassell: 1958) has suggested that the worshippers of Dionysus ate mushrooms. The *amanita muscaria* gave them great physical strength so that they were able to tear animals to pieces, and the *panaellus papilionaceus* induced 'harmless and most enjoyable hallucinations'. To discuss the correctness of Robert Graves' theory is not in my province. I used it because it fitted my own way of looking at the myth. Apollonian man makes logical connections, directs his attention outwards, regards others as part of a complex network of social obligations, remembers the past and plans for a likely future: he is the centre of his own world, to be sure, but there is a world for him to be the centre of. Dionysian man (or woman) is the opposite, and the experience provided by the hallucinatory drugs, and particularly L.S.D. *is* opposite: it is private and sensual, and the connections it makes are imagistic, having nothing to do with verbal logic. Where others do enter the experience, they do so in a Dionysiac way, and the experience becomes a group-experience, as panic is, not a cooperative experience as a committee is. Therefore 'We eat mushrooms'. Therefore the lack of communication when the women try to explain to Pentheus what the experience is like. 'Under the hallucinatory drugs, disassociation of perception is a common phenomenon,' he says: he has an intellectual understanding but he cannot share. And when he is torn to pieces, he still cannot understand what is happening.

It may be objected that those who speak with missionary zeal about the 'mind-opening' qualities of L.S.D. are notoriously pacifists. They tell us that they hate war, and they have not yet been known to tear royalty to bits. But first we should note that to hate war is not the same as hating violence. To wage war means to accept social organization. An army is one of the most intricate social organizations there is.

Secondly, one must remember that to tear someone to bits need not imply the intention to cause pain. Once the concept of cause and effect has gone, the concept of cruelty has gone. Let us take a sequence of events. An arm is pulled off a body. Pretty blood appears, and can be smelt. A noise is heard. Logical Apollonian man calls the noise 'screaming', and makes the connection between the statements, but to a mind that doesn't use logic, they may only be statements of sensation.

You may think it unfair to hippies that I should associate them so firmly with L.S.D., when it is unlikely that all hippies, or even most hippies, take it. But I needed an equivalent to the Bacchae which should both fit the myth and be recognizably a part of our own world in 1969, and the philosophy of the hippies is private, is interior, is anti-social and anti-logical, and does include an approval of the hallucinatory drugs. There is also another way in which hippy life fits the myth. Hippies are not rationalists. They are usually religious people, though their religion is not Christianity, or any other institutionalized religion. Indeed, to talk to a hippy about religion at all is likely to be confusing to a logical person, but what will probably emerge is a mish-mash of Hindu religious philosophy, in which the most outstanding idea is that, 'God is in everything. Everything is good.'

The hippies, then, get their religious ideas from the East – and Dionysus-worship came to Greece out of the east. Again one may object that (leaving L.S.D. out of the account this time) the belief that 'Everything is good' is innocent and peaceful, not at all violent. 'Everything's good. Morning's good. Food's good. Hot's good. Cold's good. Naked is good. Flowers are good. Shit's good.' – how does this end with tearing someone to pieces? Only extend it – 'Pain's good. Killing's good.' Then we remember that Kali is as much a part of Hindu religious belief as Krishna, and our Apollonian heads may feel a little less secure on our shoulders.

I have suggested (on p. 12) that the argument of the play has three points of view. Again I looked to the myth to provide me with a third protagonist. The view is taken in dialogue by the Senior Departmental Secretary, but the real protagonist does not appear in the play, though his shadow lies heavily over it. This is Echion, the king's father.

The city of Thebes, as the myth has it, was founded by Cadmus, a grandson of Poseidon. The Delphic Oracle told him to follow a cow until she lay down, exhausted, and there to build a city. So he found a cow, and followed her for a long time, and at last she inconsiderately chose to collapse near a spring which was guarded by a dragon. This dragon killed most of Cadmus' soldiers, after which he himself killed the dragon, and was ordered by Athene to plant the dragon's teeth. He did so, and a new army of soldiers grew from the teeth, and at once fell to fighting each other until only five survived. To one of these five, Echion, Cadmus married his daughter Agave.

In fact the myth does not tell us that Echion ever ruled Thebes: Cadmus resigned his kingship directly to his grandson. But I have chosen to depart from the myth, and for two reasons.

The first is contained in a speech of Pentheus to Dionysus in Act One.

'My father was a soldier, and I am told, a good one. *He* was the law here in Thebes. Its strength was his strength.

The city was young, and needed such strength. I honour him. But needs change.'

The reign of Echion stands for a period in the evolution of states which is, of course, longer than the lifetime of one ruler, just as the reign of Pentheus does. The play reminds us that, although states may evolve from such a form of government, they also revert to it, as my city of Thebes is clearly in for another bout of Echion-rule when the play ends.

This is a general statement. Plays may make such statements, but actors cannot act in general terms; they need particularities. So there is also a particular reason for my use of Echion, and it is to do with the characterizations of Pentheus and Agave, and the narrative development of the play. There had to be a reason within his own character why Pentheus should dress up as a woman, and go to the mountain to spy. There had to be a reason below the ostensible reason that she sees only crouching bones and thinks them to be those of a lion, why Agave should tear him to pieces. There had to be something in them both for Dionysus to work on, something that belonged particularly to him.

An actor begins by asking, 'Who am I?' – perhaps that is why so many plays deal with what is called 'the problem of identity'. Suppose we begin by saying to Pentheus, 'You are a king. You are an only son, and unmarried. Your father was a warrior. You believe in peace, in tolerance, in equality under the law, and that those who live under the law should share in making it.' The actor playing Pentheus, the actress playing Agave, certainly the director, must ask, 'Why an only son? Why unmarried?' By asking questions of this sort, always with reference to the text itself, they will be able to find the basis of a sub-text out of which the characterizations will grow.

Such a sub-text will begin with Echion, a rough violent man, an absolute king, who gets one son on his wife, and no healthy children thereafter. He finds his pleasure elsewhere, in the company of soldiers, the practice of war, the enjoyment of easy sexual conquests, leaving her largely without pleasures. The son is taken early from his mother to be taught to be a king, and reared in a manly way. Agave has been deprived of a child, Pentheus of a mother. He grows to hate his father. More than that, he grows to fear his father in himself, for he knows himself to be his father's son – lust, violence, selfishness, these are his father's characteristics, which he must fight against, both publicly as a ruler and privately within himself. When his father dies, Pentheus has been planning for a long time to reverse his father's policies, and does so.

One might expect mother and son now to be reunited, but this would be to ignore the passage of twenty years. There is a six-year-old Pentheus inside Pentheus which longs for its mother – lusts after her, indeed: Oedipus may not have had an Oedipus-complex, but Pentheus certainly does. But lust must be denied, childishness cannot be acknowledged. As for Agave, she is presented with a well-meaning stranger in his early twenties when what she wants is the six-year-old who was taken away. And in place of the isolation she suffered under Echion, she is presented with the obligations of a Queen Mother in a constitutional monarchy. It is just as lonely, more restricting, and with as little of any real importance to do.

Since Dionysus is a god, we may assume that he knows the sub-text: so he has quite enough to work on in persuading the characters to destroy themselves. And if anyone should object that, as a god, he should not need to work, that a single miracle of some cataclysmic sort should be enough to punish Thebes without putting him to the trouble of impersonating a man and all that follows, then I should answer that the gods do impersonate men (Christ did, for one), and that trapping someone into destroying himself seems to be a favourite method of destruction with them. As for miracles, though they have nearly all been supplied with a rational explanation, I have kept one, which is not in the myth: it is my own small miracle. The music which calls the women to the mountains comes out of the air, and is never explained. I've already remarked that E. Nesbit was my favourite author when I was a child. I enjoy magic, particularly in the theatre.

London, April 1969   JOHN BOWEN

B

A first draft of this play was performed by third-year students of the London Academy of Music and Dramatic Art in June 1968. The first professional production was at the Stables Theatre Club, Manchester, on February 19th, 1969, with the following cast.

FIRST WOMAN SECRETARY AND FIFTH WOMAN	Maureen Lipman
JUNIOR DEPARTMENTAL SECRETARY	Richard Howard
SECOND WOMAN SECRETARY	Carla Challenor
SENIOR DEPARTMENTAL SECRETARY	Robert Morris
PRINCIPAL PRIVATE SECRETARY	André van Gyseghem
FIRST WOMAN	Celia Hewitt
SECOND WOMAN	Ann Rye
AGAVE	Maureen Pryor
THIRD WOMAN	Marion Winton
PENTHEUS	William Roache
FOURTH WOMAN	Vivienne Davies
POLICEMAN	William Simons
DIONYSUS	John Fraser

The play was designed by Christopher Hewitt, lit by André Tammes and directed by the author.

Act One

The actual set will vary according to the type of theatre in which the play is to be played. At the L.A.M.D.A. theatre, where I directed a draft of the play, the audience was in the smaller segment of a circle, with the front row of the audience on the same level as the floor of the stage. At the Stables Theatre Club, Manchester, a traverse stage was used, with the audience on opposite sides and the action between them. Even a picture-frame stage could be used provided that there were some kind of apron to allow the actors to make direct contact with the audience from time to time.

What is essential is that there are three platforms, connected to each other, and each higher than the one before. These represent the administrative offices of the city of Thebes. The top platform is the office of King PENTHEUS, *the middle the office of certain* DEPARTMENTAL SECRETARIES *and the king's* PRINCIPAL PRIVATE SECRETARY. *The lowest platform is where the* WOMEN SECRETARIES *sit.*

A second essential is a reasonably spacious flight of steps. Where the audience sits in front of the action, these steps can be leading up to the administrative offices. Where a traverse stage is used, the steps are opposite the offices with what is assumed to be a piazza in between. In that case, the steps lead up to a statue of Apollo which is part of the exterior of the City Art Gallery. This separation of steps and offices can also, of course, be used on a stage of any shape.

The offices are pastel grey. The desks will need to be small so as to allow as much free movement as possible, and will be relatively uncluttered. Each desk has a touch of red: this will most usefully be provided by a red egg-lamp, extended when the desk is occupied, down when it isn't. The king's office has the largest desk, and a swivel-chair, and an extra chair for visitors. Outside the offices, all is clean and bright and functional.

Although whatever is used must work, the set is not naturalistic. No walls divide the offices, and one can speak from the top office down to the piazza if circumstances demand it.

There is no curtain. Before the play begins, the set is lit with whatever pre-set lighting the director thinks suitable. All desks are unoccupied.

Fade to black-out. During the black-out, the theme music of the play is heard. I myself have used the verse and first chorus of a recording by the Manfred Mann Group, My Name is Jack.

Lights on the lower platform. The FIRST WOMAN SECRETARY *enters, and goes to her place, noticing that the other desks on the platform are empty. She extends her egg-lamp and is preparing to start her working day when Music is heard – the music of a distant flute or piccolo and drum.*

The music affects her. She is fascinated by it, begins to decide to follow it, then changes her mind as the music stops.

The JUNIOR DEPARTMENTAL SECRETARY *enters, and lights come up on the middle platform as he goes to his desk. Conversation as he passes.*

JUNIOR SECRETARY. Good morning.

FIRST WOMAN SECRETARY. Good morning.

During the conversation, the SECOND WOMAN SECRETARY *enters. She also notices an empty desk on the lower platform.*

SECOND WOMAN SECRETARY. She's not back yet?

FIRST WOMAN SECRETARY. No.

The SENIOR DEPARTMENTAL SECRETARY *enters, and goes to his desk. Exchange of* 'Good Mornings' *as he passes the two* WOMEN SECRETARIES, *who do not much like him.*

SENIOR SECRETARY (*to* JUNIOR SECRETARY). Good morning.

JUNIOR SECRETARY. Morning.

As the SENIOR SECRETARY *is about to sit, the music is heard again. Both* WOMEN SECRETARIES *react to it. Then the* FIRST WOMAN SECRETARY *contracts her egg-lamp, and is clearly about to leave.*

SENIOR SECRETARY. Er . . .

SECOND WOMAN SECRETARY. You off?
FIRST WOMAN SECRETARY. Thought I might. (*She goes off.*)
SENIOR SECRETARY. Thirty-six.

Lights up on the ground area, as the PRINCIPAL PRIVATE
SECRETARY *enters and speaks to the audience.*

PPS. Here in Thebes, we run an orderly city,
    Each day decently divided, the weeks divided, each year
        divided,
    Work and recreation, a time and place for each,
    To each family a home, and a share in our good city,
    In our City Hall, Art Gallery, Museum, Public Library,
    In our Civic Theatre, Ice Rink, Hospitals, University,
    In our Public Parks, where daffodils are planted every Spring
    Where crocuses bloom, and each in their regular seasons
    Tulips, roses, chrysanthemums,
    Are planted, and bloom, and are lifted before they die,
    Each making room for the next in orderly progression.

A telephone rings on the desk of the SENIOR SECRETARY *and is
answered.*

SENIOR SECRETARY. City Government. Department of Sani-
    tation ... Yes? ... Yes? ... Oh, no. No question of that.
    It's all reprocessed, madam, before you drink it ... Not at
    all. My pleasure, madam. Goodbye. (*He puts the phone down.*)
PPS. Here in Thebes, there is social security.
    Children are educated, and the mentally ill are cared for.
    The old are filed away in almshouses, where they can be
        with each other.
    Coloured people are integrated. We have one-way traffic
        and clean air.
    And the orderly process of government goes on from day
        to day.

Phone rings on the desk of the JUNIOR SECRETARY *and is
answered.*

JUNIOR SECRETARY. City Government. Department of Family
    Welfare ... Yes? ... Surely that's a Police matter. Missing
    Persons is a Police matter, sir. I'm afraid we – Oh, did you?

Just a moment, please. (*He puts his hand over the mouthpiece, to speak to the* SENIOR SECRETARY.) Another one gone.

SENIOR SECRETARY. Oh dear! Wife and Mother or Young Person?

JUNIOR SECRETARY. Wife and Mother. Two children at school. This is the husband.

SENIOR SECRETARY. Well, cope, my dear fellow. Cope.

The JUNIOR SECRETARY *continues his phone call.*

JUNIOR SECRETARY.. I'm so sorry ... Yes, clearly they must be fed. They'll have School Dinners, of course; that should hold them till this evening. Have you tried the GPO Dial-a-Recipe Service? ... No, I don't – Sir ... I am trying to cope. I am trying to cope ... (*Angry.*) Then go out and get some chips, why don't you? ... I said, 'Chips'. C for – (*Clearly the caller has hung up.*) Helpless idiot!

The SENIOR SECRETARY *gets up. He looks down at the lower platform.*

SENIOR SECRETARY. 'Chips'! Working-class, I take it. And consequently domestically helpless. *My* father wouldn't push a pram, you know. He wouldn't even push *me* in a pram. I was a pretty child. I suppose that embarrassed him.

The SECOND WOMAN SECRETARY *notices him looking at her, and smiles and waves. He returns to his seat.*

JUNIOR SECRETARY. She's still there, then?

SENIOR SECRETARY. Yes.

PPS. Here in Thebes, we are a tolerant community.
  We take a mature view. We respect the individual.
  Eccentricity of behaviour, eccentricity of belief, of worship
    are all allowed.
  Chapel and synagogue stand side by side,
  Mosque and temple and Oddfellows Hall.
  Freedom of expression, it's cardinal: we cherish it here.
  Pornographic pictures and books are freely sold,
  And public speakers in Constitution Square
  Hire portable platforms from the park attendants,

Advocating Anarchism, Constitutional Monarchy, Flat
    Earth, Progressive Socialism,
Fascism of all sorts, Peace, a Businessmen's Government.
Speaking without censorship to a heterogeneous audience
Of hecklers, tourists, and those who are merely out
For a little surreptitious groping on a sunny Sunday.

The music of a flute and drum is heard from offstage.

   He reacts to it. The SECOND WOMAN SECRETARY'*s head
turns sharply to listen. Both* DEPARTMENTAL SECRETARIES *are
clearly made nervous by the music.* A WOMAN *enters from the
direction of the music. She has long hair, wears 'beat' clothes,
carries a shoulder bag. The* PRINCIPAL PRIVATE SECRETARY
looks at her, and she meets his glance frankly.

WOMAN. I love you.
PPS. Thank you.

*She reaches the steps and makes herself comfortable, still watched
by the* PRINCIPAL PRIVATE SECRETARY. *She takes a string of
worry-beads from her shoulder-bag, and begins playing with them.
The* PRINCIPAL PRIVATE SECRETARY *decides to continue
addressing the audience.*

We are a proud people in Thebes. We have a right to be.
Setting as we do an example to civilized states.

*The music begins again offstage, from a different direction. Since
this is also the direction in which he knows the* WOMAN *is sitting,
the* PRINCIPAL PRIVATE SECRETARY *turns swiftly to catch
her at it. But she is only playing with her worry-beads. The*
SECOND WOMAN SECRETARY *and the* TWO DEPARTMENTAL
SECRETARIES *have reacted to the music as before. The* PRINCI-
PAL PRIVATE SECRETARY *goes to the* WOMAN.

PPS. Excuse me?
WOMAN. You're excused.
PPS. Was that you?
WOMAN. Was what me?
PPS. Making that noise?
WOMAN. Noise?
PPS. Music.

WOMAN. Oh . . . the music.

PPS. Were you making it?

WOMAN. You heard music?

PPS. Distinctly. I heard the music of a distant drum. A fife and drum.

WOMAN. What's a fife, for God's sake?

PPS. A piccolo.

The WOMAN *shrugs: clearly he must be crazy. The* PRINCIPAL PRIVATE SECRETARY *controls his irritation.*

A flute.

WOMAN. Oh! You heard a flute?

PPS. And drum. I heard a flute and drum.

WOMAN. Distant, though.

PPS. I asked you, Did you make it?

The WOMAN *opens her shoulder-bag to show him its contents.*

WOMAN. Where's my flute? Where's my drum?

He begins to move away. The WOMAN *calls him, and he stops.*

Hey!

PPS. Yes?

WOMAN. 'Fife': I like that. It's good. I like that a lot. I'll remember that. 'Fife'.

PPS. Thank you.

Music again. The SECOND WOMAN SECRETARY *stands up to listen. The* JUNIOR SECRETARY *looks at her.*

Battle of looks. She is defeated, and sits again. The PRINCI-PAL PRIVATE SECRETARY *moves in the direction of the music, trying to place it. As he moves away from the* FIRST WOMAN, *a* SECOND WOMAN *comes from upstage left, and joins the* FIRST WOMAN. *She also takes worry-beads from her bag, and begins to play with them. Music stops. Then it starts again.* PRINCIPAL PRIVATE SECRETARY *turns sharply. He sees that there are now two* WOMEN. *Pause. He approaches them.*

May I ask what you are doing here?

SECOND WOMAN. Watching the people.

PPS. There are no people.

SECOND WOMAN. There will be.

Defeated, he turns back to the audience.

PPS. We live under the law in Thebes.

The music starts again. The PRINCIPAL PRIVATE SECRETARY *gives up his attempt to address the audience. He turns to go to his office. Then he sees* AGAVE, *the queen, who is walking towards the direction of the music. She is a middle-aged, upper-class lady, with blue hair, very much the Queen Mother. The* PRINCIPAL PRIVATE SECRETARY *is horrified.*

Oh my God!

She ignores him. He attempts agitatedly to stop her, without actual physical contact.

Ma'am . . . If you please, ma'am . . . Ma'am, if you would be guided by me . . . Oh, ma'am, pray consider the effect on public opinion. Do nothing rash . . . (*As she goes.*) Don't go . . .

AGAVE. So kind, so kind . . .

AGAVE *goes off, pausing only to make little royal hand-gestures at the audience. The* PRINCIPAL PRIVATE SECRETARY *turns back to the* WOMEN.

PPS (*angry: despairing*). That was the king's mother.

They look at him.

What are you *doing*?

SECOND WOMAN. Sitting on the steps.

They return to their worry-beads. A THIRD WOMAN *enters. She approaches the* PRINCIPAL PRIVATE SECRETARY, *takes a handful of petals from her shoulder-bag, and throws them over him. Then she settles herself with the others.*

The PRINCIPAL PRIVATE SECRETARY *sneezes.*

THIRD WOMAN. No love in your heart, friend?

PPS. Vegetation gives me hay-fever.

FIRST WOMAN. But we love you.

PPS. I don't care.

He leaves them, and goes to his office on the middle platform. But as he reaches the lower platform, he realizes that there is a woman missing. He says to the SECOND WOMAN SECRETARY:

Where? – Oh, never mind.

He continues to his own office. The DEPARTMENTAL SECRE-TARIES *stand as he arrives.*

A terrible thing has happened. We must all be calm.

JUNIOR SECRETARY. Fifteen this morning. So far.

SENIOR SECRETARY. It's containable. It's a containable problem.

JUNIOR SECRETARY. It's an epidemic.

PPS. Take a grip on yourselves.

They do.

The Queen Mother has gone with them.

SENIOR SECRETARY. With whom?

PPS. Up ... Up there. Wherever they go. Mount Cythaeron. She passed me. 'Ma'am,' I said. 'Pray consider.'

SENIOR SECRETARY. Consider the effect!

PPS. My very words. She never answered, never even paused. She took no notice. She went on.

JUNIOR SECRETARY. But graciously.

PPS. Oh, affably. She smiled and waved, as she went.

JUNIOR SECRETARY. Every inch a royal.

PPS. That's not the point. She's gone.

SENIOR SECRETARY. Attended?

PPS. Alone.

JUNIOR SECRETARY. She won't be alone for long. (*To the* SENIOR SECRETARY.) 'Containable,' you said.

SENIOR SECRETARY. One couldn't know it was coming under royal patronage. Of course, there have been signs. She went to rather a daring play last month. Royalty should stick to musicals.

PPS. She wasn't even dressed for mountain sports.

SENIOR SECRETARY. What do they do, exactly?

Pause.

PPS. I don't think we need bother our heads about that.

PENTHEUS *enters. He sees the* WOMEN *on the steps.*

PENTHEUS. Good morning.

SECOND WOMAN. Morning's good.

PENTHEUS. Yes, isn't it. (*To the* SECOND WOMAN SECRETARY *as he reaches her.*) Good morning.

SECOND WOMAN SECRETARY. Good morning. (*Stands.*)

PENTHEUS *notices the empty desks.*

PENTHEUS. Ill?

WOMAN SECRETARY. Absent, your Majesty.

PENTHEUS. I see.

He continues to the second platform. All stand.

PPS. Your Majesty, I regret . . .

PENTHEUS. My mother? I know it.

SENIOR SECRETARY. And fifteen others so far today, Your Majesty.

JUNIOR SECRETARY. Twelve yesterday.

SENIOR SECRETARY. Nine the day before.

JUNIOR SECRETARY. Thirty-six in all.

SENIOR SECRETARY. Thirty-seven with her Royal Highness.

Music starts again, this time down left, off. The SECOND WOMAN SECRETARY *stands.*

PPS. No!

PENTHEUS. She's a free agent, as we all are.

PPS. But in office hours, sir!

PENTHEUS. Remind her.

PPS. Excuse me, miss. The day is not over. Are you taking a break?

WOMAN SECRETARY. I'm sorry, Mr Secretary. Something's come up.

PPS. But you can't just go. You have to have permission.

WOMAN SECRETARY. Please may I have permission to go?

PPS. No. Permission is not granted.

WOMAN SECRETARY. Pity. Goodbye all.

PPS. You'll be dismissed.

WOMAN SECRETARY. Why should I worry? We've got Full Employment in Thebes.

PENTHEUS. Let her go.

The SECOND WOMAN SECRETARY *goes off.*

JUNIOR SECRETARY. Thirty-eight.

PENTHEUS. Who makes the music?

PPS. One is never sure.

SENIOR SECRETARY. They have a leader, sir.

JUNIOR SECRETARY. We don't know if he's musical.

PPS. In any case, there's no direct cause and effect. It's not like the Pied Piper of Hamelin. If it were simply the music, then all the women would go. Or all who were going, would go at once. But some women go when they hear it. Some go later. Some don't go at all.

SENIOR SECRETARY. Most don't. Viewed statistically, those who go are a very small proportion of the total female population.

PENTHEUS. A proportion which grows, however. Mr Secretary, shall we go into my office?

The SENIOR SECRETARY *gives the* PRINCIPAL PRIVATE SECRETARY *a file. The* PRINCIPAL PRIVATE SECRETARY *and* PENTHEUS *move onto the upper platform. Lights come up on it.* A FOURTH WOMAN *comes from downstage to join the other three.*

SECOND WOMAN. Did you get anything?

FOURTH WOMAN. No, they don't like beggars. They've got that National Assistance scene here.

SECOND WOMAN. That's a good scene.

PENTHEUS. Please sit, Cadmus. (*The* PRINCIPAL PRIVATE SECRETARY *moves the chair near* PENTHEUS' *desk.*) I spoke to my mother. I asked her not to go.

PPS. So did I. That is, I suggested that not going might be a more suitable course of action for Her Royal Highness. Or, strictly speaking, a course of inaction. She ignored me.

PENTHEUS. Yes; she does that. Though you could hardly threaten my mother with the sack.

PPS. No, I couldn't.

PENTHEUS. There's no reason why they shouldn't go, of course. If my mother, or any other woman in the city over the age of consent, should decide to take a little holiday in the mountains, she's entitled to do so. It's not a crime to leave one's family to look after itself.

PPS. Unless very young children were left unattended.

PENTHEUS. Have any very young children been left unattended?

PPS (*consults file*). No.

PENTHEUS. Can you think of a single reason for stopping them?

PPS. Something general. The public good?

PENTHEUS (*irritated*). What good? You said yourself, young children are not left unattended. There's Miss Thing gone in the lower office.

PPS. Three gone, sir. Three of them.

PENTHEUS. Very well; there's absenteeism in the Public Service. It's not a crime. The workers of this city have a right to withdraw their labour. Anything else would be intolerable.

PPS. Very well, sir. Public order.

PENTHEUS. Who says they're disorderly? (*No reply.*) Have there been any reports of disorder? (*No reply.*) Of incitement to disorder, even? This man, this leader . . .

PPS (*consults file*). Dionysus of Lydia.

PENTHEUS. Does he incite anyone to disorder? Riot? Defacement of public property? Litter? Has he so much as persuaded a dog to foul the pavement?

PPS. He's persuaded Her Majesty, the Queen Mother, to climb Mount Cythaeron.

PENTHEUS. Dammit, we don't *know* that. We only know she's done it.

PPS. He says he's a god.

A POLICEMAN *enters. He stands looking at the* WOMEN *on the steps.*

PENTHEUS. It's not a crime. It's not even enough to get him

committed to a mental institution. Believing oneself to be a god is eccentricity. Of course if one goes about smiting people with thunderbolts, that's another matter. (*Pause.*) What do you think they do, exactly?

PPS. Do?

PENTHEUS. Up there. On the mountain.

PPS. Oh . . . female things.

PENTHEUS. What sort of female things?

POLICEMAN. Come along. Move along there, please.

FIRST WOMAN. Why?

POLICEMAN. Never mind the questions, madam. Just move along, please.

SECOND WOMAN. We're not doing anything, just sitting on the steps.

THIRD WOMAN. We can sit. Anyone can sit.

POLICEMAN. Obstruction.

SECOND WOMAN. We're not obstructing anyone.

POLICEMAN. You're obstructing me for a start, aren't you?

THIRD WOMAN. From what?

POLICEMAN. From moving you on.

PENTHEUS. Do you know, women sometimes tell each other dirty jokes? It's hard to imagine a thing like that. I mean, one knows objectively that they may, but it's hard to imagine one's own mother and sister doing it. Using the words.

PPS. My mother's dead.

PENTHEUS. And mine is halfway up Mount Cythaeron. What about those women on the steps?

PPS. I've instructed the police to lean on them.

PENTHEUS. Why?

PPS. They're not residents.

PENTHEUS. So?

PPS. One doesn't want aliens, hanging about the public parks and buildings, watching the people.

PENTHEUS. Mr Secretary, that is what tourists do.

POLICEMAN. Come along now. I told you to move on.

FOURTH WOMAN. Where?

POLICEMAN. Anywhere. Just keep moving.

At a signal from the SECOND WOMAN, *the* WOMEN *rise, take one step to the left and sit again. All smiling.*

FOURTH WOMAN. We moved.

PENTHEUS. First. We don't know there's a problem. The women may return at any time. Furthermore, as your colleague pointed out, only a small proportion of the women of Thebes have gone to the mountain.

PPS. There's discontent, Your Majesty. In the city.

PENTHEUS. They have husbands. Why don't the husbands fetch them back?

PPS. They seem to think it's up to the government to do something about it.

PENTHEUS. Then why haven't we sent anybody from Family Welfare?

PPS. We have.

PENTHEUS. And?

PPS. Most of our Psychiatric Social Workers are women, as Your Majesty knows. Those we sent didn't come back.

Pause.

PENTHEUS. Very well. If there is a problem, what is its nature?

PPS. My colleague suggested an epidemic.

PENTHEUS. Illness?

PPS. Mental illness.

PENTHEUS. Which is not infectious, Cadmus.

PPS. Hysteria is.

PENTHEUS. Ah!

DIONYSUS *enters. Unlike the* WOMEN *who lean to scruffiness,* DIONYSUS *dresses attractively – perhaps all in white – and should be beautiful. The* WOMEN *see him before the* POLICEMAN *does.*

SECOND WOMAN. It's the man.

Ad libs – 'Hi!' 'That's him' – general greetings from the WOMEN *so that the* POLICEMAN *turns to look. The* FIRST WOMAN *throws him an orange, which she takes from her shoulder-bag. This is in fact a made-up orange which contains a mushroom for reasons which will appear.* DIONYSUS *stands there, playing with the orange, looking amusedly at the* POLICEMAN, *who is discomforted.*

PENTHEUS. You say he claims to be a god, this man?

PPS. In a manner of speaking.

PENTHEUS. People actually worship him?

PPS. Up to a point.

PENTHEUS. They worship him or they don't. He's a god or he isn't.

PPS. He says everyone's a god. Everyone should be worshipped.

Down below, the POLICEMAN *tackles* DIONYSUS.

POLICEMAN. And what do you think you're doing?

DIONYSUS. Standing.

POLICEMAN. You've got nothing better to do, I suppose?

DIONYSUS. No.

POLICEMAN. Well, you can't stand around here. We don't allow it.

DIONYSUS. Standing?

POLICEMAN. Loitering. It's not permitted.

THIRD WOMAN. It's all right if you move.

FOURTH WOMAN. We just moved.

FIRST WOMAN. He likes you to move.

SECOND WOMAN. He watches.

DIONYSUS. Well . . . moving's good.

SECOND WOMAN. Standing's good.

THIRD WOMAN. Sitting's good.

FOURTH WOMAN. Being's good.

FIRST WOMAN. Yes, that's best. (*To the* POLICEMAN.) Being is best.

POLICEMAN. It's not a question of what's good. It's a question of . . . (*Fades out.*)

DIONYSUS. A question of what?

FIRST WOMAN. A question of moving.

SECOND WOMAN. Well . . . moving's good.

POLICEMAN. It's a question of public order.

DIONYSUS. I don't see anyone else moving. If everyone in the city kept moving the whole time, you'd be bound to notice it.

THIRD WOMAN. They move in their homes.

FOURTH WOMAN. From room to room.
FIRST WOMAN. Running on the spot.
SECOND WOMAN. Stops you from having a coronary.
DIONYSUS. So you don't want a coronary.

The WOMEN *begin to move around the* POLICEMAN. *Uneasy, he moves away. They are dancing and touching him, singing,* 'Coronary! Coronary!' *He panics, and pulls out his gun.*

POLICEMAN. Stop!

All stop suddenly. The POLICEMAN *backs away from the group of* WOMEN, *still menacing them with his gun. The* FIFTH WOMAN (*double for* FIRST WOMAN SECRETARY) *enters from behind him. She tilts his cap forward on his head. As he whirls round, half-blinded and confused, she strokes his gun in a sexually suggestive way. All the* WOMEN *laugh. Then joined by the* FIFTH WOMAN *they group themselves again on the steps by* DIONYSUS.

DIONYSUS. Enough movement?

The POLICEMAN *decides, after uncertainty, to seek further instructions.*

POLICEMAN. Excuse me. You stay there.
DIONYSUS. Don't worry. We shan't move.

The POLICEMAN *goes to the first platform, and is surprised to find nobody there.*

POLICEMAN. Er . . . (*He goes to the second platform and coughs.*)
SENIOR SECRETARY. Come in.
POLICEMAN. If you'll excuse me.
JUNIOR SECRETARY. There's nobody in the outer office.
POLICEMAN. I've been assigned to the women.
SENIOR SECRETARY. On the mountains?
POLICEMAN. On the steps. I was assigned to lean on the foreign women, on account of they were without visible means of support.
JUNIOR SECRETARY. So you leaned, and they fell over.
POLICEMAN. No, sir. They remain immovable. I was instructed to make my report direct.
SENIOR SECRETARY. Very well. Make it.

C

POLICEMAN. I've just made it.

SENIOR SECRETARY. Thank you.

POLICEMAN. Consequently I await instructions.

PENTHEUS. As I take it, Mr Secretary, there are two groups
of women. One is a group of foreigners – religious persons
without visible means of support, on whom the police, at
your instructions are leaning. And they have a leader,
Dionysus of Thing.

PPS. Lydia.

PENTHEUS. Lydia. The second group consists of women from
our own city – citizens, with the rights of citizens. They are a
statistically unimportant proportion of the population, which
nevertheless, as you remind me, is growing. These women –
our women – suddenly down tools.

PPS. Tools?

PENTHEUS. You know what I mean. They leave their jobs and
homes, and take off for Mount Cythaeron, for an indefinite
period. Your hypothesis is that they may be mentally ill.
Mad, in fact.

PPS. Deranged.

PENTHEUS. Music is sometimes heard, but we do not know
that the women respond to it. This music, you suggest, is
somehow associated with the first group of women, and
particularly with their leader, but we never actually see them
or him making it. There is, in fact, no real evidence to
connect the first group with the second group at all.

PPS. Presumptive evidence.

PENTHEUS. What presumptive evidence? There's no evidence
the man makes the music; there's no evidence the music
makes our women leave. Where's your presumptive evidence?

PPS. The music has only been heard since his arrival, Your
Majesty. And the women have only been leaving since the
music began.

PENTHEUS. It's not a logical connection. You talk about epi-
demics. If there'd been an outbreak of cholera, would you
say there was presumptive evidence, that this man had
caused it?

PPS. Yes.

Pause.

PENTHEUS. Why?

PPS. He upsets people.

PENTHEUS. What people?

PPS. Me! (*Pause.*) If it were cholera, I'd inspect the water supply, to be sure, but I'd also deport the man. (*Pause.*) Your Majesty, the man is an alien. He has no civil rights here. He can't go to law over a deportation order.

PENTHEUS. The man is a man. That gives him rights.

PPS. It's a problem of public order, Your Majesty. We have a duty to be safe. There's discontent in the City.

PENTHEUS. We have no duty to ignore our own consciences. Without cause, we can neither stop the women going, nor deport the man. They have free choice, and he has broken no law.

PPS. And if all our women should go? (*Pause.*) Your Majesty.

PENTHEUS. They haven't.

PPS. Your Majesty spoke of logical connections. They might all go. Even if fifty per cent were to go –

PENTHEUS. It's not likely.

PPS. What proportion would have to go before Your Majesty considered the matter serious enough for official action? I wish for guidance here.

PENTHEUS. That will do.

PPS. I say again, 'Your Majesty spoke of logic.' If Your Majesty sees no reason in conscience to stop one, surely there would equally be no reason to stop two thousand. Contrariwise, –

PENTHEUS. You go too far.

PPS. I have a conscience also. (*Pause.*) I fail to understand why Your Majesty is reluctant to act.

FIRST MALE SECRETARY. You'll have to wait. I can't interrupt him. He's with His Majesty.

PENTHEUS. Very well. I'll see the man.

PPS. But there's no occasion –

PENTHEUS. I'll see the man.

Pause. The PRINCIPAL PRIVATE SECRETARY *leaves the upper*

platform. Meanwhile the FIFTH WOMAN *has risen to her feet. One of the* WOMEN *has brought on a bongo (the* THIRD *or* FOURTH WOMAN *probably), and* DIONYSUS *taps out a rhythm for dancing. Other* WOMEN *hum the tune while the* FIFTH WOMAN *dances. The noise should be muted until the* POLICEMAN *leaves the offices, then sharply increased in volume.*

PPS. Ah, constable!
SENIOR SECRETARY⎫ This fellow seems –
POLICEMAN.   ⎭ According to instructions –
PPS. The king will see the man. Bring him here.

PENTHEUS *has come to the top of his steps.*

PENTHEUS. Ask him to come.
PPS. Ask him to come.
POLICEMAN. He's outside, Your Majesty. They're all outside. Sitting.
JUNIOR SECRETARY. Convenient.
PPS (*looking down at the dancing*). Sitting!
PENTHEUS. Ask him now.

The POLICEMAN *goes down to the steps.*

POLICEMAN. You're to see His Majesty.
PENTHEUS. Sit there. (*To the* JUNIOR SECRETARY, *pointing to centre desk.*)

The dance continues.

POLICEMAN. Well, come along. Don't hang about.
PENTHEUS. Question him. I'll observe.

He takes the vacant desk, and the PRINCIPAL PRIVATE SECRETARY *takes his place on the steps.*
The dance finishes.

DIONYSUS. We're to see the king.
POLICEMAN. Not all of you. Just him. (*To the* WOMEN.) You wait here. (*To* DIONYSUS.) You come with me.

They go to the first platform. DIONYSUS *takes in, with pleasure, the fact that the office is empty.*

DIONYSUS. Nobody home?
POLICEMAN. That way.

DIONYSUS *comes to the second platform. The* POLICEMAN *moves back to a position where he can keep an eye on the* WOMEN.

PPS. Good morning.

DIONYSUS. Morning's good.

PPS. I wish to ask you some questions.

DIONYSUS. You mean you wish me to answer some.

PPS. Precisely. You are Dionysus?

DIONYSUS. Yes.

PPS. Of Lydia?

DIONYSUS. Of everywhere.

PPS. What?

DIONYSUS. I'm Dionysus wherever I am.

PPS. But recently of Lydia.

DIONYSUS. Of Thebes at the moment. I live where I am.

PPS (*consults file*). When questioned by the Department of Immigration, –

DIONYSUS. That's right. There was a man at the gate, asking questions.

PPS. A routine matter. The same for everyone. There was no unfairness or preferential treatment.

DIONYSUS. He was older than you. Depressed. 'Where do you come from?' he said. 'Lydia,' I said. In Lydia they said, 'Where do you come from?' I said, 'Thrace,' In Thrace, they said –

PPS. Thank you.

DIONYSUS. But you have more questions than they had in Lydia; I will say that. And more depressed people.

PENTHEUS. The people of Thebes are not depressed.

DIONYSUS. Well, *you* know . . . Grey.

Pause.

PENTHEUS (*to* PPS). I'm sorry. I interrupted.

PPS. Dionysus, there is the question of your religious views. Have you anything to say on that?

DIONYSUS. What's the question?

PPS. What *are* your religious views?

DIONYSUS. I don't have views. I just have religion.

PPS. You confused the officer. At the gate.

DIONYSUS. That's right; I did. 'Name?' he said. 'Dionysus,' I said. 'Religion?' he said. 'Dionysus,' I said. He got confused. (*To* PENTHEUS.) Grey, but confused.

PPS. Please explain your religion.

DIONYSUS. Nothing to explain. I am my religion.

PENTHEUS. Please don't evade the question. The gentleman is not trying to trap you. There is no religious persecution in Thebes. We have agnostics ... atheists ...

SENIOR SECRETARY. We like to make provision for minority interests.

DIONYSUS. Interests?

SENIOR SECRETARY. Convictions. Any sort of convictions. Religious. Political. Social.

JUNIOR SECRETARY. Vegetarian Restaurants. Crematoria.

DIONYSUS. Lovely teeth!

JUNIOR SECRETARY. Foreign films.

DIONYSUS. Oh ... you'll make provision for me?

PPS. Indeed yes.

PENTHEUS. Just tell the gentleman what facilities you require.

PPS. For instance, if you were musical at all. If music played an important part in your services ...

DIONYSUS. I don't hold services.

PPS. But you must.

DIONYSUS. Why?

PPS. You can't have a religion without services, however informal. You have to worship something; that's what service means. A service of worship.

DIONYSUS. Some thing?

PPS. Some god. Some abstract principle. Some idea. Some symbol. Something has to be worshipped.

DIONYSUS. Yes. Me.

PPS. You have to be worshipped?

DIONYSUS. Yes.

PPS. Then somebody has to do the worshipping.

DIONYSUS. Yes. Me.

PPS. You worship you?

DIONYSUS. Yes.

PPS. And those women on the steps? Whom do they worship?

DIONYSUS. Me.

PPS. Ah! Do they . . .

DIONYSUS. And I worship them. It's very simple. I worship me, and they worship me. I worship them, and they worship them. Suppose you wanted to worship with us. You'd worship me and them and you. And I'd worship you and me and –

PPS. When everyone worships everyone, there is no worship.

DIONYSUS. Oh there is. The best sort. You should try it.

PENTHEUS. What do you do? Exactly.

DIONYSUS. We worship.

PENTHEUS. At your worship, what do you do?

Pause.

DIONYSUS. We eat mushrooms.

Pause.

PPS. That's all?

DIONYSUS. That's the main thing.

PPS. It sounds . . . very innocent.

DIONYSUS. It is.

PPS. *I* eat mushrooms. I like them.

DIONYSUS. Good . . . Good. Eating mushrooms is good.

PPS. With bacon for breakfast.

JUNIOR SECRETARY. With steak and kidney in a pie.

DIONYSUS. That's good. That's very good.

SENIOR SECRETARY. Champignons à la grecque.

JUNIOR SECRETARY. Sliced in a cream sauce with veal.

DIONYSUS. Good. Champignons and veal is good.

PENTHEUS. He means a special sort of mushroom, I think. (*Stands.*) And there's what you've been looking for, Mr Secretary. Drugs.

He descends to ground level. (If the WOMEN *are sitting on the steps leading up to the offices, he will have to push through them, saying, 'Excuse me.') The* POLICEMAN *steps forward.*

PENTHEUS. It's all right, officer. (*Speaks to the* WOMEN.) Tell me what happens when you eat the mushrooms.

DIONYSUS *has followed* PENTHEUS *down. The* WOMEN *ignore*

PENTHEUS *and look at him.* DIONYSUS *speaks in his own good time.*

DIONYSUS. Tell him.

The scene which follows was called 'Psychedelia' in rehearsal: all four of the WOMEN's *group-scenes had names. It is important to remember that the* WOMEN *are not high. They have two objectives. One is to discomfort* PENTHEUS. *The other is to explain to him what the LSD experience is like. They work as individuals, speaking sometimes to* PENTHEUS, *sometimes to the audience (to whom they are also explaining). The scene has much movement.*

FIRST WOMAN. We hear colours.

SECOND WOMAN. Red. (*Repeats the word, fading it away under the next line.*)

THIRD WOMAN. Green. (*Same treatment of the word.*)

FOURTH WOMAN. Ultramarine. (*A shout.*)

FIFTH WOMAN. I hear a snake on a rock.

    Green rubbing on black rock.

The FIFTH WOMAN *has become a snake as she speaks, and is rubbing herself against* PENTHEUS' *legs, so that he moves embarrassedly away. And so on for the rest of the 'Psychedelia' scene.*

FIRST WOMAN. A sunset, an ape's behind: it's like an explosion.

SECOND WOMAN. I hear the sky.

    The great blue bowl of the sky shouts and echoes.

    I bounce off the blue of the sky like a rubber ball.

FOURTH WOMAN. *Bounce*-ie. *Bounce*-ie.

SECOND WOMAN. I feel the sky. I rub it between my fingers.

    I rub the clouds between my fingers until they squeak.

THIRD WOMAN. We hear colours. We see sounds.

DIONYSUS. They hear colours, and see sounds.

PENTHEUS. Disassociation of perception. That happens.

DIONYSUS (*enunciates*). Dis-association.

THIRD WOMAN. Trucks bumping.

    Tubs and trucks, bumping and thumping.

    Black coal falling, bump! bump!

FIRST WOMAN. Black. Bump!

The SECOND *and* FIFTH WOMEN *take up* 'Bump! Bump!'
repeating it, while:

FOURTH WOMAN. Dis-ass-oh-see-eh-shun.

The THIRD WOMAN *takes up* 'Disassociation', *repeating it. So
we have three women repeating* 'Bump' *while two repeat* 'Disassociation'. DIONYSUS' *interruption cuts them off sharply.*

DIONYSUS. Of perception.

FOURTH WOMAN. Per *cep* shun.
  Cep shun.
  Cep ... cep ... it's lonely. Shun: it's lonely.
  It's cold here.
  No fur. Dead eggs. Stones.
  Cold stones.
  Per-cep-shun.

PENTHEUS. Under the hallucinatory drugs, disassociation of
  perception is a common phenomenon.

FIFTH WOMAN. I feel time. I walk through time like treacle.
  The seconds are sticky on my skin.

SECOND WOMAN. I have a fawn in my lap.

THIRD WOMAN. Brown. Dappled brown, clattering.

SECOND WOMAN. The fur is alive, each hair alive.
  Each hair prickles against my fingers.
  Each hair is a fawn, licking and sucking my fingers.

FOURTH WOMAN. Per *cep* shun.
  Dis ... dis ... disassocate.
  Dissassssss!

FIRST WOMAN. I know the meaning. What it means. What all
  means.

FIFTH WOMAN. The meaning of all. The meaning of nothing.
  The meaning.

FIRST WOMAN. Not in words, not sounds, not scents.

FOURTH WOMAN. Scent! Scent!

FIRST WOMAN. The meaning is the meaning.
  Not sights. Not feeling.

FOURTH WOMAN. Feeeeeeeling!

FIRST WOMAN. Everything clear in light with clear edges.
  The meaning.

Everything bigger, bigger, expanding, filling.

FIFTH WOMAN. Everything smaller, smaller, disappearing into the meaning.

FIRST WOMAN. The meaning into the meaning.

SECOND WOMAN. The feeling into the feeling.

THIRD WOMAN. Sounds within sounds of colours within colours.

Colours unimaginable, never invented, never yet heard.

The colours of meaning.

FOURTH WOMAN. Meeeeeeening!

All the WOMEN *speak at once, the* FIRST *and* FIFTH *to* PEN-THEUS, *the other three to the audience, shouting out the names of colours and the sounds of sounds.* PENTHEUS *has to shout.*

PENTHEUS. Enough! I've heard enough.

They take no notice of him.

DIONYSUS. Enough.

Noise cuts out at once. The WOMEN *return quietly to their places. It is the end of 'Psychedelia'.* DIONYSUS *peels the orange he has been holding, and reveals that it contains a mushroom. He gives this to the* FIRST WOMAN *as a prize.*

FIRST WOMAN. Does he understand?

DIONYSUS. No.

PENTHEUS. I understand enough.

DIONYSUS. Enough to clear your conscience?

PENTHEUS. Now you're impertinent.

DIONYSUS. You want to deport us, but you needed a reason. Now you think you have a reason.

PPS. There is a reason. Drugs! It's despicable. There's never been a problem of addiction in Thebes.

DIONYSUS. Mushrooms aren't addictive. Perceptive maybe.

FIRST WOMAN. Yes. We feel perception. To know. Everything opening.

PENTHEUS. Perception can also be addictive, I think. (*Going up to his own office.*) Mr Secretary, will you please deal with this matter in accordance with the laws of the city?

DIONYSUS. And the women on the mountain?

PENTHEUS (*stops*). What?

DIONYSUS. I noticed that your man asked me if I'm musical.

PPS. 'Man'! Don't call *me* 'man', my man.

DIONYSUS. Aren't you a man? You look like one. Wait! – don't tell me. You cater for minority interests.

PENTHEUS. What *about* the women on the mountains?

Music heard. The FIRST *and* SECOND WOMEN *leave, following the music. It stops.*

DIONYSUS. But I don't, you observe, make it.

PPS. Not directly. No.

DIONYSUS. Magic?

PPS. Don't be ridiculous.

PENTHEUS. Do you admit a connection between yourself and the women on the mountains?

DIONYSUS. Why shouldn't they go to the mountains.

PENTHEUS. Do you admit a connection?

Music heard again from a different direction. The THIRD *and* FOURTH WOMEN *follow it.*

SENIOR SECRETARY. That came from a different direction.

JUNIOR SECRETARY. They went off a different way.

DIONYSUS. There are many different ways to the mountain. You should be more concerned with why they go than which way they choose.

PPS. We know why they go. You . . . (*Discovers he doesn't know how to finish the sentence.*)

DIONYSUS. What?

PPS. I don't know what you do. You do something.

DIONYSUS. Your father would not have needed an excuse to get rid of me.

PENTHEUS. Do you admit a connection between yourself and the women on the mountain?

DIONYSUS. Your father would have put me in prison, or banished me, or had me killed. It would have been all one to him.

PENTHEUS. We have changed that.

DIONYSUS. Yes, you look for excuses. It seems a little shabby.

PENTHEUS. We look to the law. My father was a soldier, and I am told, a good one. *He* was the law here in Thebes. Its strength was his strength. The city was young, and needed such strength. I honour him. But needs change. At first, simply to be alive, to have food and shelter and company, is most important for men. But these are an animal's needs, and we are more than animals.

DIONYSUS. More? Or less?

PENTHEUS. We have intelligence, forethought and memory. We perceive harmony, and respond to logic. We have compassion and concern: we care for each other. What must the law do, then, but help us to be the difference between men and animals – to be most truly ourselves? Such laws cannot depend upon the strength of one man. Our strength is in the laws themselves. They are made by all men together, in free argument and persuasion. Those who break the laws must be punished, for they have broken the strength of our city, but none may be punished who has not broken the law. I am the servant of the law: my crown is the badge of my service. I do not look for excuses, Dionysus. I measure you against the law, and it seems that you may have offended.

DIONYSUS. How?

PPS. By being in possession of certain substances. The law is clear.

PENTHEUS. Drugs diminish a man. Our laws help men to be themselves.

DIONYSUS. And if I say they do not diminish men?

PENTHEUS. I have told you what makes a man. Intelligence. Co-operation. Concern. Respect. What isolates a man, diminishes him. What makes him a danger to his fellows diminishes him. What impairs his judgement diminishes him.

DIONYSUS. And the women on the mountain? – since we must return to them. You asked if I admitted a connection. What sort of connection have you in mind?

Pause.

SENIOR SECRETARY. I suppose . . .

PENTHEUS. Yes?

SENIOR SECRETARY. If he were a pedlar. A dope-pedlar.

JUNIOR SECRETARY. A pusher.

PPS (*to the* POLICEMAN *who goes to obey*). Keep an eye on that woman. (*To* DIONYSUS.) Trafficking in substances. There are very heavy penalties.

SENIOR SECRETARY. Unless he were a doctor, supplying substances under prescription. Then no offence would have been committed at all on either side.

PPS. Do you hold a degree in medicine?

DIONYSUS. I have no academic qualifications of any sort.

PPS. Oh, good.

DIONYSUS. You said 'on either side'. Do you punish those who buy as well as those who sell?

PPS. Of course.

JUNIOR SECRETARY. Unless they're under age. Have you been pushing substances to teenagers?

DIONYSUS. As I understand it, His Majesty's mother has gone to the mountain.

PPS. Oh, blast!

DIONYSUS. You saw her go. Did she seem drugged?

PPS. She was the picture of affable condescension.

DIONYSUS. Sloshed, you mean?

PPS. No.

PENTHEUS. I don't believe you sold my mother drugs.

PPS. But, Your Majesty, the man himself admitted –

PENTHEUS. He has admitted consuming some sort of hallucinatory drug as part of a religious ceremony. That brings him within the scope of our laws. It doesn't, however, as he reminds us, explain the women on the mountain.

DIONYSUS (*to the others*). Observe. (*He goes over to the* POLICEMAN.) You're a countryman, aren't you?

POLICEMAN. I'm a policeman.

DIONYSUS. Your father was a shepherd.

POLICEMAN (*wary*). Yes.

DIONYSUS. An ignorant man.

POLICEMAN. My father had the qualifications of his profession as I have mine.

DIONYSUS. Suppose His Majesty were to order you to arrest the women?

POLICEMAN. I should obey instructions.

DIONYSUS. Go out, and bring them in. Then His Majesty can find out for himself what connection I have with them.

Pause.

POLICEMAN. Bring all of them in?

DIONYSUS. I imagine that one would do.

Pause.

POLICEMAN. I have no jurisdiction outside the city.

DIONYSUS. But if His Majesty ordered –

POLICEMAN. His Majesty wouldn't order. I have no jurisdiction. It's a military matter.

DIONYSUS. Interesting.

The POLICEMAN *is plainly frightened, and is looking, scared, at* PENTHEUS.

(*To the* SENIOR SECRETARY). Would *you* go?

SENIOR SECRETARY (*surprised*). If His Majesty instructed me.

DIONYSUS. Yes. You're not a countryman.

PENTHEUS. Explain.

DIONYSUS. Oh . . . country legends. One doesn't necessarily believe them. An intelligent man takes everything into account, of course. Allowing it its own weight, no more.

PENTHEUS. What legends?

POLICEMAN. If Your Majesty has no further instructions, the termination of my term of duty is approaching.

PENTHEUS. Please stay. (*To* DIONYSUS.) What legends?

DIONYSUS. About women who go to the mountains. Thessaly isn't far away. There are stories which the country people know. Peasants.

PENTHEUS. My mother is not a peasant, Dionysus. The women from this office who have gone are not peasants, but educated women.

PPS. Social workers have gone. Women with university degrees.

DIONYSUS. What did you cut off, then, when you educated
   them? (*To* POLICEMAN.) Tell His Majesty your story.
PENTHEUS. Speak freely.
DIONYSUS. I shall help you.
POLICEMAN. It is a story they tell in our village.
   The people are not educated there. Most cannot read.
   Our entertainment, sirs, is telling stories
   And dancing sometimes or singing. No harm is meant.
   As for the stories, one has to say they're true
   Or nobody would listen.
   But they're all remembered matters. No one was ever there.
   They wouldn't stand up as evidence.
PENTHEUS. And this story?
DIONYSUS (*prompts*). It was dawn.
POLICEMAN. It was dawn –
   The way they tell it, it was dawn. They tell it
   Of another village over another hill.
DIONYSUS. It was dawn.
POLICEMAN. The early sunlight was warming the rocks.
   Cowherds – the people of the story – peasant people – cow-
      herds and shepherds –
   They were taking out the animals to graze
   Upon the mountain meadows.
   And came upon the women.
PENTHEUS. What women?
POLICEMAN. Dancing women.
PPS. Dancing?
POLICEMAN. Not at the time, sir; no. They were at rest.
   But dancing women is what the stories call them.
   Now they were tired. They lay about in sleep,
   Some with heads back, arms wide, legs stretched apart,
   Since there was no man near to take advantage.
   Some lay like dolls dropped by a child in haste,
   Some close with fingers touching, some cuddled up
   To a tussock of grass or a heather clump.
   It was pretty to see them, the stories say, so open and
      innocent.
PENTHEUS. No great harm in this.

DIONYSUS. More follows.

POLICEMAN. Then their leader –
They have a leader always –

DIONYSUS.   – the stories say.

POLICEMAN. Someone of . . . (*Falters.*)

PENTHEUS. Yes?

POLICEMAN (*miserable*). Someone of noble blood, Your
Majesty.

DIONYSUS. Nothing democratic. They prefer royalty
If they can get it.
Otherwise a duchess, countess, even a marchioness,
A lady J.P. in the remoter regions.
But an acknowledged leader, nobody elected.

PENTHEUS. Go on.

POLICEMAN. Their leader heard the sounds the cattle made
And gave a cry to rouse them all from sleep.
So they rose up, rubbing the sleep from their eyes,
Tousled and fresh from sleep as the fresh morning air,
Old women, young, wives and unmarried girls.
Their hair was loose, flopping about their shoulders.
They wore tunics of dappled fawnskin, laced with thongs.
But some, instead of leather thongs used snakes,
Live snakes which licked their cheeks and lips as they moved.

PPS. Disgusting!

POLICEMAN. Mothers, whose babes were left behind at home –

PPS. Aha! You see! Children left unattended.

POLICEMAN. Mothers whose babes were left behind at home.
Held tiny fawns and wolfcubs to their breasts
To ease them of their milk, and there they suckled.
The women's hair was wreathed with leaves,
Tendrils of ivy and white-flowering bryony.
All carried stalks of fennel, and one struck
Her staff against a rock, whereat a fountain
Of water bubbled out. Another wanted wine
And found a spring of wine among the moss,
And many others scratched the soil for milk,
Scrabbling the roots of heather with their fingers,
And from the soil white milk came spurting up.

Their food was honey which dripped from the tips of
    their wands.

PPS. This is preposterous.

DIONYSUS. Exaggerated perhaps.

PPS. Honey from sticks!

JUNIOR SECRETARY. A sticky secretion?

PPS. That will do, Themistocles!

PENTHEUS. How far were these herdsmen from what you have
    described their seeing?

DIONYSUS. The stories don't go in for that kind of detail.

PENTHEUS. Continue.

POLICEMAN. The herdsmen wondered at these miracles,
    Questioning and arguing amongst themselves.
    Until one fellow, bolder than the rest,
    Said, 'Since these women live as beasts,
    And beasts untended must be free to all,
    We'll lay an ambush, hide among the leaves,
    Spring out and capture some fine female hind,
    Use her, and let her go. She'll take no harm,
    Since beasts are common in concupiscence
    And made for use. What an advantage here,
    To use a beast, yet do no bestiality!
    Sure, we should take it.' So we hid ourselves, –

PENTHEUS. 'We?' 'Ourselves?'

DIONYSUS. No, he is re-living the story. If you interrupt him,
    he'll forget.

POLICEMAN. *They* hid *them*selves,
    Leaving their animals to wander free,
    And watched the women. So often men may see
    A herd of deer graze on a grassy plain.
    Movement within the group, yet the group still.
    You watch. You note the markings of each animal.
    See here an ear twitch, there a scabby flank.
    One shits profusely. Another cannot settle,
    Searching for juicier grass while others crop.
    Watching, you give them names.
    'There's Reckless, Droopy Tits, and this one's Agnes.'
    Just so the herdsmen watched, and each man marked

D

His private favourite whom he hoped we'd catch.
So might an hour pass, or a day, or a minute,
But on some signal or a sudden start
Your herd becomes again a single thing
Like water flowing, or a gust of wind,
The separate parts now altogether lost
In running, leaping, dancing unity.
And so it was. Suddenly the women ran.
Running was all around us. In the air.
We were engulfed in it. The very mountain
Seemed as if it would run with the running women.
So that we held –

PPS. We!

POLICEMAN. The herdsmen held each other.
Each, since he could not trust himself, must force his fellow
To stay in stillness, to resist the tide,
And lie in ambush for the women.
And then there came the first, the lady leader,
And leaping up, the herdsmen tried to seize her.
'Bacchae!' she cries, 'Bacchae! Hounds that hunt with me!
Here are men – men come to hunt *us* down.
Strike! Strike them down with your wands.'
The women were terrible. Wild. Snakes writhed on their
    necks and shoulders.
Their hair wild. Their hair like nets.
Their eyes red and terrible, their sticks suddenly sharp,
Tearing and piercing flesh. The herdsmen ran,
And the women laughed, and ran on, on into the meadow,
Where our fat cows fed. They did not need spears then.
They tore the cattle with their hands.
A proud bull, lowering his head to charge, was torn apart,
Stripped of flesh and skin. Heifers were clawed in pieces.
And the women ran on.
They ran, flew like great birds.
Blood was under their nails, and running down their arms.
Blood was in their mouths like wine. Down, down the
    mountain they ran.
They came to the village.

He breaks down, and cannot continue.

PPS. It is . . . only a story, you know.
DIONYSUS. Tell it to the end.
POLICEMAN. They took children, took them where they were,
  Babies from their cradles, little boys hiding,
  Frightened children, hiding behind their mothers.
  These women who had suckled wolves at their own breasts
  Took human children, and tore them into pieces.
  And when the village people tried to fight,
  Men of that village who were not cowards, sirs, only
    frightened,
  When they took up spears, knives, swords to protect their
    children,
  Pointed sharp spears toughened by fire,
  The spears drew no blood from the women,
  But the women's sticks killed.
  A stalk of fennel could spill a man's guts as he fought for
    his child.
  In the end, all ran.
  The village burned. The women returned to the hills.
  They washed their hands in the clear mountain springs,
  And the snakes licked the blood from their cheeks.

Pause.

PENTHEUS. My mother is with those women.
PPS. Your Majesty . . .
PENTHEUS. Yes?
PPS. With your permission . . . if I may submit . . .
PENTHEUS. Yes.
PPS. It is only a story. The man wasn't there.
SENIOR SECRETARY. Hearsay.
JUNIOR SECRETARY. Legend.
PENTHEUS (*to the* POLICEMAN). You may go.
DIONYSUS. Go now.

The POLICEMAN *goes.*

SENIOR SECRETARY. Honey from sticks!
JUNIOR SECRETARY. Water from rocks!
SENIOR SECRETARY. Milk from mother earth!
JUNIOR SECRETARY. Snakes in the hair!
SENIOR SECRETARY. Oh, it's your full mythological armoury.
PENTHEUS (*to* DIONYSUS). Please come with me.

DIONYSUS *follows* PENTHEUS *to the top platform, while:*

PPS. Thank you for your kind co-operation, gentlemen.

Subdued, the DEPARTMENTAL SECRETARIES *return to their desks. While:*

PENTHEUS. Please sit.

DIONYSUS *sits. During the scene which follows, he will, since* PENTHEUS *is restless, find the opportunity to change places, so that he sits at the king's desk in the king's chair.*

What do they do up there?
DIONYSUS. You heard the man.
PENTHEUS. Can one believe him?
DIONYSUS. No. It was only a story.
PENTHEUS. But you knew it. You knew it before he told it.
DIONYSUS. I've heard it before. I travel about.
PENTHEUS. Do you believe it?
DIONYSUS. I'd want to see for myself.

Pause.

PENTHEUS. If it were true!
DIONYSUS. There'd be a scandal.

Pause. PENTHEUS *looks at him.*

PENTHEUS. How very silly you must think me!
DIONYSUS. Please! Please!
PENTHEUS. No administration wants a scandal, and as you so
    cheerfully point out, my own family is involved. But that's
    the least of it.
DIONYSUS. I'm sorry.
PENTHEUS. We make a good life for our people here. I tried
    to make you understand that. Nothing in excess. Every-

thing in moderation. Everything works. Everyone has a part
to play in the life of the city. Balance. Equality. Freedom
under the law. Respect. Even those who do the dirtiest and
most monotonous jobs have compensation and respect.

DIONYSUS. A noble ideal!

PENTHEUS. Yes. A reasonable society. It's not exciting, but it
is noble. Only – occasionally something happens which dis-
turbs me. Something irrational. Violent. Wanton damage to
public property. The tyres of vehciles slashed at night. A
small boy, sent out to get the groceries for his mother, is set
upon in the open street, and left with a broken arm and eggs
in his hair. I try to understand that kind of thing. I *don't*
understand it, but I try. If the offenders are caught, they
receive psychiatric help instead of punishment. Often they
are not caught, because the offence is motiveless.

DIONYSUS. You do believe the story, then?

PENTHEUS. No, it's a legend, as you say.

DIONYSUS. If it were true . . .

PENTHEUS. It couldn't be true. Wooden wands that pierce
flesh like spears! Women giving suck to snakes! It couldn't
be true.

DIONYSUS. Suppose the things that could be true, were true.
And all the rest had a rational explanation. Then what?
(*Pause.*) Suckling snakes *could* be true.

PENTHEUS. Tearing cattle to pieces!

DIONYSUS. Could be true.

PENTHEUS. Strangling children!

DIONYSUS. Could be true. Most of the story *could* be true.

PENTHEUS. I asked you, do you believe it?

DIONYSUS. I told you, I'd want to see for myself. (*Pause.*) Or
if *you* believe it, then call out the Military Reserve. The
Police Force. Bring the women in. You could have special
arrangements for making sure Her Royal Highness isn't
recognized. An overcoat over the head is usual; it annoys
the photographers. (*Pause.*) If the bit about the sticks turning
to spears should be true, there might of course be bloodshed.

PENTHEUS. You said . . . You're sitting in my chair.

DIONYSUS. Yes.

Pause.

PENTHEUS. You said you'd want to see for yourself?

DIONYSUS. That was my advice. No need to take it. (*Pause.*)
But if you knew – if you actually knew what they did –
exactly, then you'd know how to act.

PENTHEUS. What they did?

DIONYSUS. It could be innocent. A little sunbathing. Euryth-
mics. Mountain walks. If you'd called out the Armed Forces,
and all you found when you got to the mountain was a Keep
Fit Class, you'd never hear the end of it. But on the other
hand, if there were anything . . .

PENTHEUS. Anything?

DIONYSUS. Goings-on. If there were anything actually going-
on. Goings-on going-on, as one might say.

PENTHEUS. But there are no men.

DIONYSUS. Herdsmen? Enormous illiterate peasants with
equally enormous equipment. Who's to know? Who'd tell?

PENTHEUS. But they're old women, some of them. Past the
change. My mother –

DIONYSUS. You know these illiterate peasants. They're not
choosy. Give them somewhere to put it, and a bit of a
wriggle once it's in, and –

PENTHEUS (*shouts*). Be quiet! (*Pause.*) I'm sorry.

DIONYSUS. Of course, for really wild goings-on, they wouldn't
need men at all. They've got each other, and lots of animals.
Snakes. Just imagine what you could do with a co-operative
snake.

PENTHEUS. I am . . . imagining it.

DIONYSUS. I see you are.

PENTHEUS. How would . . . I mean, if I wanted to . . .

DIONYSUS. Watch?

PENTHEUS. See for myself. What happens.

DIONYSUS (*gets up, and comes to him*). That's the point, how
to do it. A helicopter? No, you wouldn't get close enough.
Anyway, they're so noisy. Disguise is best.

PENTHEUS. Dress up as a peasant?

DIONYSUS. It's a thought.

PENTHEUS. A smock? Corduroy trousers, tied at the knees
   with string?

DIONYSUS. Not trousers.

PENTHEUS. Why not?

DIONYSUS. Are they going to let a man get near them? I only
   ask.

PENTHEUS. Then?

DIONYSUS. You'll have to go in drag.

PENTHEUS. I don't understand you.

DIONYSUS. As one of them. Dress as a woman.

Pause.

PENTHEUS. But I don't . . . look like a woman.

DIONYSUS. Make-up? A wig? Powder down all that butch
   stubble.

PENTHEUS (*angry*). I do not resemble – I do not in any way
   resemble a woman.

DIONYSUS. No. You do not. No. (*Pause.*) Pity. (*Pause.*) I tell
   you what. That secretary down below, the pretty one with
   the teeth. Let him go. He'd drag up lovely.

He comes to call to the JUNIOR SECRETARY.

   Hey, you! Pretty boy with the teeth! Come on up to His
   Majesty. And bring my dolly lady with you.

JUNIOR SECRETARY. Well!

The three of them look at each other.

PPS (*to the* JUNIOR SECRETARY). Go on.

The JUNIOR SECRETARY *does so.*

   I'll bring the woman.
   He goes to lower level and says to the FIFTH WOMAN.
   Please come here. I'm taking you to His Majesty.

DIONYSUS. You're to drag up.

JUNIOR SECRETARY. You're joking.

SENIOR SECRETARY. What would you like *me* to do?

PPS. Wait here. (*Takes the* FIFTH WOMAN *on up to the top
   platform.*)

PENTHEUS (*to the* JUNIOR SECRETARY). Put your clothes on that chair.

PPS. The woman!

PENTHEUS. Thank you. Please wait outside.

PPS. Oh! (*He goes back to his own desk, and sits.*)

DIONYSUS (*to the* FIFTH WOMAN). You don't mind changing clothes? With him.

FIFTH WOMAN. Changing's good.

She strips off her outer garments. The JUNIOR SECRETARY *is appalled.*

PENTHEUS. Well, go on! Go on!

The JUNIOR SECRETARY *reluctantly takes off his jacket, and begins to remove his shoes. The* FIFTH WOMAN *has stripped down to some pretty ratty underwear.*

FIFTH WOMAN. Strip right off?

PENTHEUS. No! (*Pause.*) No, thank you.

FIFTH WOMAN. He should hurry. I'm cold.

DIONYSUS. Cold's good. Hot's good; cold's good.

FIFTH WOMAN. Cold's cold, though.

SENIOR SECRETARY. What do you think they're doing up there? Exactly.

PPS. His Majesty is devising a plan.

SENIOR SECRETARY. What sort of a plan?

PPS. To deal with the women on the mountain.

The JUNIOR SECRETARY *has removed waistcoat, tie and trousers.*

JUNIOR SECRETARY. Your Majesty . . .

PENTHEUS. Yes?

JUNIOR SECRETARY. I wear . . . very little underwear. I'm embarrassed.

PENTHEUS. Are you trying to tell me you don't wear any?

JUNIOR SECRETARY. No, no! I do wear underwear, Your Majesty. It would be very insanitary to wear none at all. It's just that there's not much of it.

PENTHEUS (*control*). Please take off your shirt, and put on the woman's . . . er . . .

DIONYSUS. Gear.
PENTHEUS. Gear.

The JUNIOR SECRETARY *takes off his shirt and is revealed as wearing black bikini-type underpants. The* FIFTH WOMAN *hurriedly begins to dress in his clothes.*

DIONYSUS. Very pretty.
FIFTH WOMAN. Good legs.
DIONYSUS. What do you care? You've been with some very draggy people.
FIFTH WOMAN. Oh . . . legs are good.
PENTHEUS. Put on the gear.

The JUNIOR SECRETARY *grabs her clothes and puts them on quickly.*

JUNIOR SECRETARY. Your Majesty, why?
PENTHEUS. Intelligence work.
DIONYSUS. Heavily disguised, you will penetrate the enemy lines, gather intelligence, and return to make your report.
JUNIOR SECRETARY. What intelligence?
PENTHEUS. What they do.
DIONYSUS. Exactly.
PENTHEUS. Walk!
JUNIOR SECRETARY. What?
PENTHEUS. Walk. I want to see you walk.

The JUNIOR SECRETARY *walks.*

PENTHEUS. No. It's unconvincing.
DIONYSUS. Ungraceful. (*To the* FIFTH WOMAN). Show him.
FIFTH WOMAN. Walk?
DIONYSUS. Walking's good.

The FIFTH WOMAN *walks in front of the* JUNIOR SECRETARY.

PENTHEUS. Copy her.

He does so, overdoing it.

Don't waggle your behind like that. It's suggestive.
JUNIOR SECRETARY. Sorry.
DIONYSUS. It's meant to be suggestive.

PENTHEUS. Oh . . . (*To the* JUNIOR SECRETARY.) Very well. Waggle your behind, but don't overdo it.

DIONYSUS. You are brutal with him.

JUNIOR SECRETARY. Your Majesty . . . what am I to do?

PENTHEUS. You are to go, disguised, to Mount Cythaeron, observe the behaviour of the women, find out what exactly they are doing and with whom – whether there is, for instance the smallest grain of truth in that ridiculous story we heard – and then return to report to me.

JUNIOR SECRETARY. I'm to join them?

PENTHEUS. Observe them. But closely. I shall go with you part of the way. Proceed.

DIONYSUS (*to the* FIFTH WOMAN). Proceed, Euphrosyne.

The FIFTH WOMAN, *followed by the* JUNIOR SECRETARY, *followed by* DIONYSUS *and* PENTHEUS, *descend the stairs. The* PRINCIPAL PRIVATE SECRETARY *stares uncomprehendingly.*

PPS. Er . . .

SENIOR SECRETARY. Oh, Themistocles!

DIONYSUS. We're doing a recce on the mountain. His Majesty will remain at Base Camp One while your friend makes the final ascent to the summit, where he will plant a flag on the Queen Mother.

PENTHEUS *hears this. It throws him. They have descended to ground level.*

PENTHEUS. I heard that. I didn't like it. First, you suggested that I would send a subordinate into greater danger than I am prepared to face myself.

DIONYSUS. Isn't that what you're doing?

PENTHEUS. There is no danger of any kind. He will not join the women in . . . in anything they do. He will simply observe them from a safe distance.

DIONYSUS. Yes, it would be worrying if he joined in.

PENTHEUS. Second, your reference to Her Majesty, the Queen Mother – (*Breaks off.*) What did you mean, 'It would be worrying if he joined in'?

DIONYSUS. With the Queen Mother. It would be worrying if

he joined in with the Queen Mother. I mean, you'd never know he hadn't.

PENTHEUS. But he won't even *observe* the Queen Mother. He –

DIONYSUS. How can he help it?

Pause.

PENTHEUS. She won't be doing anything.

DIONYSUS. Can you be sure? Noblesse oblige, and all that. And you know what snobs women are. They'd want her on the Committee at least.

PENTHEUS. Oh!

DIONYSUS. Your father would have sent him, heard his report in private, and then had him quietly strangled.

PENTHEUS. No!

DIONYSUS. I don't suggest it. I merely make the observation. Anyway your father would have wanted to see the whole thing himself. He'd have enjoyed it. He had a taste for goings-on, as I've heard. Nothing elaborate. Just a simple gang-bang with a little sadism on the side.

PENTHEUS. I am not my father. (*Pause.*) Themistocles! We're going to the palace. I shall come with you all the way. I had better change my clothes.

PENTHEUS, *the* JUNIOR SECRETARY *and the* FIFTH WOMAN *go off.*

DIONYSUS (*speaks to the audience*). The bird is tangled now
In the fowler's net. He shall see the dancing women,
And pay for it with his life.
Already the wits of this rational king have gone wandering.
You will see him walking in women's dress.
He will make one discovery after another,
Until the last, and then none.
So shall he and you all come to know
That Dionysus, son of Zeus, is a powerful god,
Most terrifying, and yet most comforting to mankind.

Lights fade.

End of Act One

The Argument Before Act Two

During the interval, all office furniture has been struck from the top and lowest platforms. If the steps are separate from the office, then the statue of Apollo has been removed to reveal a skeletal, non-naturalistic tree, the back of which is a ladder solid enough for PENTHEUS *to climb during the action. If the steps lead up to the office, then a ladder of wood or rope, decorated with cut-out leaves, has been lowered from the flies near to the steps. In either case, the steps now represent a mountain glade.*

At the end of the Interval, the various bells or warning voices have been sounded, but the house lights are not lowered or only partially so. The WOMAN SECRETARY, *and the* FIRST, THIRD *and* FIFTH WOMEN *enter, and arrange themselves on the steps. Then, when the house is silent, the* PRINCIPAL PRIVATE SECRETARY *enters, and addresses the audience. The Argument that follows is carried on between the characters, but involving the audience as people who may take sides.*

PPS. What is understanding? What is wisdom?
 Of all human qualities, wisdom is most prized,
 And should be held in most honour.
SENIOR SECRETARY (*entering*). To be most honoured is to be
 most victorious.
PPS. No.

AGAVE *enters, and joins the* WOMEN.

SENIOR SECRETARY. To hold the fate of an enemy in your
 hand.
 When your hand is poised over the head of your enemy,
 When you strike the falling head from the fallen neck,
 When you lift the head by its hair, holding it up scornfully
  for all to see.
 Then is your power shown –

AGAVE *laughs*.

SENIOR SECRETARY. – and in power is honour.
PPS. In understanding.
SENIOR SECRETARY. In power.
AGAVE. The power of the gods is revealed when the gods will.
  Slow it may seem in action, but the gods do not keep our
    time.
  They choose their own.
  Slow as a wasting cancer, swift as an avalanche,
  Their power may be shown.
SECOND WOMAN (*enters*). The gods punish.
FOURTH WOMAN (*enters from another direction*). Punish.
SECOND WOMAN. Strike down. That is their pleasure.
  The only reward they give is not to punish.
  They strike down pride.

The SENIOR SECRETARY *laughs*.

SECOND WOMAN. They humble the proud. They accept your
    challenge
  That man who challenges the gods offers himself to their
    pleasure.
  He may charge and dodge. He may fight a long fight.
  But in the end *his* blood is on the sand, and the cheers
    are not for him.
AGAVE. Who talks of time to the gods?
  Two hundred years men toil to build a city,
  Which the gods destroy in a minute.
FIRST WOMAN. The gods are patient. They will lie long in
    ambush
  To trap the unbeliever.
AGAVE. They do not keep our time.
THIRD WOMAN. Blessed is he whom the gods love.
  He shall escape the storm at sea,
  And come home safe to harbour.
  He shall escape sickness and disability
  To enjoy the fruits of labour.
FOURTH WOMAN. Belief is good.

To hold the old beliefs,
Hold to the law that lies in the blood, the seed.
Honour strong instinct and sweet impulses.
Hold to the law that is outside law, stronger than law,
To the law that is undefined, uncodified, –

AGAVE.   – But known.
No thought or act is good that will ignore
The old traditions, the stories told by village fires,
The old fears of the oldest gods.

PPS. In wisdom is honour. In understanding, tolerance,
     rational thought.

SENIOR SECRETARY. In power.

AGAVE. In instinct.

SENIOR SECRETARY. Whom then should we honour?

AGAVE. The gods. Who win.

The lights fade. The PRINCIPAL PRIVATE SECRETARY, SENIOR SECRETARY, SECOND *and* FOURTH WOMEN *leave the stage. Theme music. Then the lights come up again on the steps, strong and golden. The* WOMEN *bask in the sunlight.*

Act Two

The women are now sunbathing. This scene we called 'Down Memory Lane'. The women are talking more to themselves than to each other. AGAVE *has a hatful of mushrooms, and is peeling them and passing them out. The* WOMAN SECRETARY *plaits a crown out of ivy.*

FIFTH WOMAN. It was always in the backs of cars. Well, there was one boy had this two-seater, but that was worse. He got his foot caught in the steering-wheel, and the horn jammed.

THIRD WOMAN. All the women ever thought about was clothes and where to get their hair done. I used to look at my mother and think, 'I could put my finger right through your face, and there'd be nothing behind it.' And the men used to tell each other dirty jokes and go about sniggering.

FIFTH WOMAN. I never enjoyed it.

THIRD WOMAN. I thought, 'My God, I'm so bored,' so I just walked out. It was two in the morning. The Ritz looked like a piece of mouldy wedding-cake, and I couldn't find a taxi. Typical really. Anyway I did get home in the end, and I changed into a pull-over and a pair of Nigel's old jeans, and hitched down to the coast.

FIFTH WOMAN. I've never been back. I never would go.

THIRD WOMAN. Christ no!

FIFTH WOMAN. People used to say, 'You're in need of care and protection, aren't you?'

THIRD WOMAN. I sent mummy a postcard from Folkestone. After all, I didn't want her going to the police. Then I latched on to something educational with some nuns, and the sort of immigration people never looked at me twice.

FIFTH WOMAN. I'd tell them, 'My mum and dad's dead.' Well, it's true in a way. Everyone's dead in our town.

THIRD WOMAN. You can get away with murder if you say you're a student.

FIFTH WOMAN. Pot and purple hearts: it was so boring.

THIRD WOMAN. Nigel got very fat-arsed after he went into the Guards.

FIRST WOMAN. That's good. Fat arses are good.

FIFTH WOMAN. The signs used to say, 'All Night Launderette' but you just try staying there all night.

The SECOND WOMAN *enters, and speaks to the audience.*

SECOND WOMAN. Elizabeth, New Jersey.

The city of Elizabeth stands on a flat marshy plain. It is an industrial city, specializing in the manufacture of pig iron. On a clear day, the skyline of New York is just visible from the city of Elizabeth. Between the skyline of New York and the city of Elizabeth there are gasometers, where the burning of waste gases makes a pattern of flame against the smoggy sky above New York. This is a view neither admired nor detested by the citizens of Elizabeth, New Jersey. They simply do not notice it.

AGAVE. When you live so much in public, you develop private vices. I used to get a sinful thrill out of picking my nose.

WOMAN SECRETARY. I never had any friends. I thought it was because I was living at home, so I had this terrible row. I mean they'd made me stay on at school, and do this secretarial course. They must have wanted me to be independent.

SECOND WOMAN. School Report. Her artistic bent is manifested in a talent for musical composition and poetry. She does not integrate fully into the group. It is possible that such overt self-isolation is an attention-getting mechanism.

WOMAN SECRETARY. Then I found I still didn't have any friends, so I realized it was just me all the time.

AGAVE. I'm not a clever woman: I don't pretend to be. I used to meet – oh everybody who mattered in the city: I had to: that was the job. They were always very careful not to talk in a clever way when I was about, in case they should say something that was above my head. They sat there, sweating out polite nothings, while I looked gracious; that made me feel very stupid. So I developed a speciality in silent farting. We Royals, my dear, we can't be noisy farters: you can understand that. But I had a way of moving one buttock very quietly. I'd sneak out great big juicy silent ones, and watch the faces. I always thought it was a mistake to play Gilbert and Sullivan at investitures.

WOMAN SECRETARY. My flat was in a basement, just off the road the lorries took to market. Every time a heavy lorry passed outside, the windows rattled. You could be listening to music or just trying to read, but you couldn't concentrate. It was a sort of vibration: your ears felt funny. I used to wash my hair nearly every evening, just for something to do.

FIRST WOMAN. Everybody selling something or buying something.

SECOND WOMAN. The subject did not undergo sexual initiation until her sophomore year at college, and since she had very little practice in dating routines, allowed her partner to go all the way. Since he was himself a mother-dominated figure with a pronounced sense of guilt, he proposed marriage, and was accepted. This was not a successful marriage.

FIRST WOMAN. If there's nothing you want to sell, and you're not in a position to buy, nobody's interested.

AGAVE. One's whole life was obligation. They called it 'duty' but it was only obligation really – a small steady drip, day after day. Being polite to people, listening, remembering names. Smiling! At night I used to have to smooth the smile out of my face before I went to bed.

WOMAN SECRETARY. There was always dust blowing in. I gave up after a bit. I mean, there's nothing to show for it, dusting. You had to keep the windows open in summer because there were hot pipes under the floor: it was to do with the central heating. All the air got dried up. I bought some freesias off a barrow on the way back from work, just for the comfort, but they were dead by morning.

AGAVE. They all used to call me 'ma'am'. Ma'am, ma'am, all the time. I wanted to say, 'You do realize "ma'am" is short for "Madam"?'

The FIRST, SECOND, THIRD *and* FIFTH WOMEN *have already*

E

been given mushrooms by AGAVE. *So has the* WOMAN SECRE-
TARY. *The* FOURTH WOMAN *comes on, and goes to* AGAVE.

FOURTH WOMAN. Ma'am?

AGAVE *looks at her, and gives her mushrooms.*

AGAVE. Here you are, sweetie. Now piss off.
FOURTH WOMAN. Pissing off's good!
AGAVE. Yes, it is.

The FOURTH WOMAN *gives a couple of mushrooms to audience.*

FOURTH WOMAN. I saw this man sitting on a bench in the
park. He kept saying, 'I'm all alone': he said it aloud. 'Nobody cares for me,' he said, 'I'm all alone in the world. I've
got nobody. I'm only fifty-four. I'm fifty-four years old, and
I'm all alone.' The people who were passing just walked on
more quickly. Me too.

WOMAN SECRETARY. I used to get nightmares, and wake up
screaming. There was a room with a glass door. It was full
of people, all waving at me. All waving. So I opened the
door, and went in to join them. The room was full of water.
The people were all drowned and dead. What I'd thought
was waving was just dead arms moving in the water.

SECOND WOMAN. Two children were born out of carelessness
and various affairs. She became a compulsive eater and
underwent psycho-analysis.

FOURTH WOMAN. 'I'm all alone,' he said, and I walked on.

WOMAN SECRETARY *passes crown to* AGAVE, *who puts it on.*
Lights fade on WOMEN. *Laughter heard.*

DIONYSUS *enters with* PENTHEUS *and the* JUNIOR SECRE-
TARY. PENTHEUS *is now in full drag with high heels and a
blonde wig. The* JUNIOR SECRETARY *also wears a wig. Both*
PENTHEUS *and the* JUNIOR SECRETARY *are giggly.* PENTHEUS
wears one high-heeled shoe and carries another.

JUNIOR SECRETARY. Oh dear! I thought we'd never get away.
(*Begins to laugh.*) And when *he* said – (*Laughter grows.*) He
said, 'How much for a stander, then?' And *you* said –
PENTHEUS. I didn't. I never did.
JUNIOR SECRETARY. Struggling with that bloody shoe.

PENTHEUS. I never. I never spoke. You are awful.

JUNIOR SECRETARY (*to* DIONYSUS). Didn't she? Didn't she say –

PENTHEUS. His face! (*They break up in laughter.*)

JUNIOR SECRETARY. She stands there, plastered with slap an inch thick. 'You're talking to a respectable married woman, my man,' she says. 'I'll report you to the admiral.'

PENTHEUS. Well, I could have.

JUNIOR SECRETARY. 'I'll help you, lady,' he says, grabbing at her foot. (*Doing so.*) 'Oooooh!' she goes. (*Laughter.*)

PENTHEUS. Stop it, stop it. I'll have an accident in a minute.

JUNIOR SECRETARY. Cross your legs, dear: it's the only way. 'A stander!' he says. And we'd been doing a hundred yards' dash till Silly Nelly gets her heel stuck in a grating. You shouldn't wear heels for the country. (*Recovering.*) Brogues: that's better. With your background, you should know. There was that lovely pair of hand-made brogues, and you wouldn't even try them.

PENTHEUS. They didn't look right. High heels stretch your calves. If you've got good legs, you might as well show them off.

JUNIOR SECRETARY. And how do you expect me to show *my* legs off, got up like a sack of potatoes. I've got better legs than you, as a matter of fact. I've had more compliments paid to my legs than you've had hot dinners, dear! Trolling along in high heels, leering at sailors! No wonder there's trouble.

PENTHEUS. I was not leering.

DIONYSUS. Girls! Girls!

JUNIOR SECRETARY (*overlaps him*). You were leering.

PENTHEUS. Smiling.

JUNIOR SECRETARY. A terrible sideways leer.

PENTHEUS. You've got to smile. Out in public, the family smiles. Smiling and waving. We're trained to do it. A gracious smile.

JUNIOR SECRETARY. Waving! Gawd, if you'd waved. Leering's bad enough.

PENTHEUS. I did not leer.

JUNIOR SECRETARY. We had to run as it was. If you'd waved,

we'd never have got rid of him. He'd have had your knickers down before you could say, 'Jack the Ripper'.

PENTHEUS. I was in control. I was totally in control.

JUNIOR SECRETARY. A wall eye, a wooden leg, three days' stubble, and a bad case of halitosis, and *she* wants to wave.

PENTHEUS. Oh come on. We'll never get there. (*Putting on the shoe.*) Sodding heel!

JUNIOR SECRETARY. Can't resist a uniform; that's her trouble.

PENTHEUS. Come on now. I've had enough of your sauce. (*To* DIONYSUS.) I've been too familiar with her, that's what it is. Give her an inch –

JUNIOR SECRETARY. An inch! I'm used to more than that, dear. (*To* DIONYSUS.) She can't resist a uniform!

PENTHEUS. Yes, I can.

JUNIOR SECRETARY. Oh, the Salvation Army – yes. The Royal Corps of Commissionaires. Boy Scouts even. But you put her within sniffing distance of the Royal Docks, and she'll be over the wall before you can say, 'Noblesse oblige'.

DIONYSUS. This way.

PENTHEUS (*as they go off*). Anyway I'm not wearing knickers. I'm not a fetishist.

Cross fade the lights to the WOMEN *on the steps. They have begun to be excited by the drug, but have not yet retreated into their private worlds. This scene was called 'Revival Meeting'.* AGAVE *is, as it were, in charge, but first the meeting is controlled by the* FIRST WOMAN, *round whom the others are grouped. As indicated the* THIRD WOMAN *later takes over the leadership, then each in turn springs into the centre, and towards the end of the scene for the first time the* WOMEN *are acting as a group, and speaking in chorus.*

AGAVE. Testify, women. Testify!

FIRST WOMAN. There was a woman with a morning appointment.

OTHERS. Yeah. Yeah.

WOMAN SECRETARY. There was a woman who cleaned the office.

OTHERS. Yeah. Yeah.

SECOND WOMAN. There was a woman in Elizabeth, New
    Jersey.

OTHERS. Yeah. Yeah.

THIRD WOMAN. Overheard on the bus.

FOURTH WOMAN. Sitting in the Underground.

FIFTH WOMAN. Next-door neighbour.

FIRST WOMAN. She said, 'I like a good laugh. I enjoy it. It
    makes the time pass.'

THIRD WOMAN. That's all they want. That's all the people
    want.

FIFTH WOMAN. That's how they live. That's how the people
    live.

FOURTH WOMAN. Making time pass until you're dead.

FIRST WOMAN. You look at the faces on your way to work.

FIFTH WOMAN. Yeah, lord. Yeah, lord.

SECOND WOMAN. If they see you looking, they look away.

OTHERS. Yeah.

FIRST WOMAN. All the dead faces, sitting in the subway,
    Passing the time from day to day.

AGAVE. Testify, women!

FIRST WOMAN. There was a man and woman sitting, opposite.

OTHERS. Oh, lord. Oh, lord.

FIRST WOMAN. Sitting side by side on a single seat.

OTHERS. Yeah, lord.

FIRST WOMAN. Bald man with a thin face, and eyes that
    blinked behind his glasses.

FIFTH WOMAN. Blink blink.

FIRST WOMAN. Thin man with a fat wife.
    Thin man with thin hair,
    Sitting there.

SECOND WOMAN. Thousands like him, sister. He's not
    remarkable.

FIRST WOMAN. Sitting there with his legs crossed, tension
    there in his hands and neck.

OTHERS. Tension.

FIRST WOMAN. She'd ask a question, then he'd nod.

OTHERS. Nod, nod, nodding his head.

FIRST WOMAN. Turned away, and nothing but nods.

And she would speak and she would say;
She'd ask a question, he'd turn away.
And so it went for the whole of the day.
Question and nod and question and blink, and question
     and question, turn away.
SECOND WOMAN. Question, question, turn away.
FIRST WOMAN. She'll go mad as he turns away.
FOURTH WOMAN. He'll go mad as he turns away.
THIRD WOMAN. They'll both go mad at the end of the day.
     All mad together and turned away.
OTHERS. That's true, sister. That's true.

The THIRD WOMAN *takes centre position.*

THIRD WOMAN. Fat-arsed Nigel and dutiful Andrew.
OTHERS. Yeah, yeah.
THIRD WOMAN. Mummy and daddy and the people in
     Dorking.
     Lie in bed late, and take the dog walking.
SECOND WOMAN. Shake it, sister.
FOURTH WOMAN. Are you saved, sister?
SECOND WOMAN. I'm saved.
THIRD WOMAN. Everyone complains that you just can't
     settle
     So you go out to coffee at the Old Copper Kettle.
WOMEN. Testify!
WOMAN SECRETARY. I wanted to meet people.
WOMEN. Testify!
FIRST WOMAN. I wanted to help people.
WOMEN. Testify!
SECOND WOMAN. I wanted to know people.
WOMEN. Yeah, yeah!
FOURTH WOMAN. People didn't want to know.
WOMEN. No, they didn't. No, lord.
FOURTH WOMAN. Grey people! Grey people!
FIFTH WOMAN. Cashier in a self-service; that's how to meet
     people.
     Hundreds and hundreds of different people.
     All different. All the same.

FOURTH WOMAN. Grey people.

FIRST WOMAN. Social work. That's how to help people.
   Hundreds and hundreds of helpless people.
   All different. All the same. All grey.

FOURTH WOMAN. Grey.

WOMEN. Faceless to the faceless.
   Anonymous to the anonymous.

FIFTH WOMAN. Behind the cash desk.

WOMAN SECRETARY. At the typewriter.

FIRST WOMAN. Behind the glass door, and the eggshell blue
   paint of the waiting-room.

FOURTH WOMAN. By the Peter Pan statue.

THIRD WOMAN. At the Commem Ball in the nasty punt.

SECOND WOMAN. Anonymous to the anonymous.
   Faceless to the faceless.

AGAVE. I was never anonymous.

FIRST WOMAN. You have to smile to give them confidence.

FIFTH WOMAN. You have to smile when you take the money.

WOMAN SECRETARY. You have to smile when they say 'Good
   Morning'.

SECOND WOMAN. You have to smile or it's un-American.

THIRD WOMAN. You have to smile or they think you're
   sulking.

FOURTH WOMAN. You haven't got a face, but you have to
   smile.

AGAVE. *I* always had a face, and *I* had to smile.
   I inclined my face to the populace,
   And I smiled, and smiled, and smiled.

ALL WOMEN. Anonymous to the anonymous.
   Faceless to the faceless.
   Dance! Run! Let the mountain dance, the forestdance!
   Now we become the mountain and the forest!
   This is a new face. This is a dancing face.
   A body that dances like the forest.
   Fawn-body, wolf-body, snake-body.

AGAVE. And a new smile for my renewed royalty.
   Nothing small. Nothing polite here.
   A wide smile to show the teeth and the red gums.

As the exhausted fox smiles at the dogs who will tear him
    to pieces,
As the wolf smiles at the terrified lamb,
As he smiles before he tears the throat of his prey,
And smiles thereafter with his muzzle bloody.
ALL WOMEN. I shall dance, leap like a fawn.
    Quick as the wind. Quicker.
    Leaping over marsh and hedge.
    Leaping for joy. Frisking.
    Dappled and free as the leaves of the forest,
    Dancing for joy in the forest.
    Far from the haunts of men.

Howling like savage animals, the WOMEN *throw themselves at*
AGAVE'*s feet. Tableau. Lights cross-fade* (*and the* WOMEN *settle
down under cover of the darkness*). PENTHEUS, DIONYSUS *and
the* JUNIOR SECRETARY *are discovered on the top platform. The*
JUNIOR SECRETARY *advances, and speaks to the audience in his
ordinary voice, with no trace of the camp of the earlier scene.*

JUNIOR SECRETARY. There were three of us made the
    journey. Pentheus and I,
    And the stranger who said he knew,
    Where the women could be found. So we left behind us
    The scattered outlying farms of the city.
    We crossed the river, and climbed the lower slopes
    Of Mount Cythaeron. We went quietly. Cautiously.
    Up gully and over scree.
    It was not easy going, dressed as we were.

PENTHEUS *is looking bedraggled, and has lost one breast. He is
trying to walk with the heel off one shoe.*

PENTHEUS. My foot hurts. I've got the most enormous blis-
    ters, hobbling along like this.
DIONYSUS. It's not much further.
PENTHEUS. I must be able to see, you know. There's not much
    point if I can't see what they do. It's all vegetation around
    here.

DIONYSUS. They usually pick somewhere open. A glade shaded by trees. Perhaps a waterfall. (*Points.*) Look!
PENTHEUS. Where?

Lights up on the WOMEN. *The* JUNIOR SECRETARY *addresses the audience.*

JUNIOR SECRETARY. We looked down. I thought we had
    found a place
Where we might spy on the women, and not be seen.
Certainly I could see them from that place.
They were in a hollow scooped out of the rock of the cliffs,
Where water ran, and pines grew in thick shade.
There they rested, innocent as it seemed to me,
They had made a crown of ivy for their queen.
Perhaps they were talking amongst themselves, singing –
    nothing of consequence,
Not what had been feared at all, not at that time.
But this was not near enough for Pentheus.
Perhaps his eyes were clouded. He could not see
The companies of women. Could not see them clearly.
Could not see, he said, exactly what they were about.
PENTHEUS. I can't see.

Light fades on the WOMEN.

JUNIOR SECRETARY. And so the two of them went on to-gether.
PENTHEUS (*to the* JUNIOR SECRETARY). You stay here.

He and DIONYSUS *move on, away from the* JUNIOR SECRETARY *who remains watching. Light fades on him.*

PENTHEUS. I'm glad we didn't bring Themistocles any fur-ther. He's clearly not very discreet. Do you really think my father would have had him strangled?
DIONYSUS. Sure of it.
PENTHEUS. Poor little love! It'd be like strangling a rabbit. Of course people *do* strangle rabbits.
DIONYSUS. And enjoy it.
PENTHEUS. All soft and helpless, and that frightened feminine look in the eye! Horrible! (*Pause.*) I don't suppose he'd

resist at all. He might squeal a bit. (*Pause.*) One has to try to understand people. If one doesn't understand a social evil, how can one hope to correct it?

DIONYSUS. We're nearly there.

PENTHEUS. We've come a very roundabout way.

DIONYSUS. We didn't want to be discovered.

PENTHEUS. My mascara's running. It'll bung my eyes up, and I shan't be able to see properly. If we just bumped into them accidently, do you think they'd know I wasn't a woman? Losing one breast in that gully hasn't helped, and of course that flat-breasted little idiot wasn't wearing any. I should have brought a spare.

DIONYSUS. I can go back and get him if you like.

PENTHEUS. What good would that do?

DIONYSUS. If you're feeling uncertain.

PENTHEUS. If you mean frightened, say so. It's no good him watching them: I'm the king. (*Pause.*) I am a little frightened, I suppose. It would be very humiliating to be ... (*Patting the solitary breast*) unmasked.

DIONYSUS. Embarrassing. Cold too.

PENTHEUS. Just tell me candidly. Do you think I'd pass?

DIONYSUS. You would. Believe me.

PENTHEUS. Would you fancy me? If you didn't know – that's the test, isn't it? If you just met me here on the mountain, all dressed up like this, would you fancy me? Would I have to run away, and break my other heel?

DIONYSUS. I'm a very fast runner. I might catch you.

PENTHEUS. Yes. (*Pause.*) You'd have a shock when you found out.

Pause. DIONYSUS *smiles slowly.*

DIONYSUS. I like one-breasted women.

Pause. PENTHEUS *nervous.*

PENTHEUS. It's lucky you know who I really am. And my voice gives me away: it broke very early, you know. We mustn't get too close. I can't see anything. Are you sure we're in the right place?

DIONYSUS. You must be patient. It's important when bird-watching.

PENTHEUS. Just like a little rabbit. I've never considered Themistocles except as a secretary. It's been a revelation today.

DIONYSUS. There's more to come.

PENTHEUS. I'm not at all shocked. And if they ... if they should suckle snakes or anything ... anything even more extreme, I shall be quite objective. Clinical. Utterly detached. I went to watch an operation once, you know. My father made me. Amputation of the leg. I fainted.

DIONYSUS. When you know what they do, you'll know how to deal with it.

PENTHEUS. Exactly. It's only a sickness really. Whatever they do, it's a sort of sickness.

DIONYSUS. That's right. You remember that.

PENTHEUS. I'm not sure I feel very well. What do you think they do?

DIONYSUS. Nameless practices. That's why they left the city.

PENTHEUS. I feel very strange. I've been feeling strange ever since I put these clothes on.

DIONYSUS. I'll go on, then, if you like.

PENTHEUS. No. I don't want *you* seeing.

DIONYSUS. I'm sorry.

PENTHEUS. I don't want just anyone seeing. You're just anyone: you know you are. And you're certainly not objective.

DIONYSUS. I am ... someone.

PENTHEUS. No, you're not. You're no one – nobody at all. If anyone's going to see my mother being ... having ... I won't have just anyone looking on. I think you forget why I volunteered for this mission.

DIONYSUS. No. I remember.

PENTHEUS. You talk about worshipping. Everybody worshipping everyone. That's what they do, isn't it? You're not a fit person. You're not objective. You won't understand it. I have a duty here, and I intend to perform it. I shall watch. I shall ... (*Stops himself.*) I'm sorry. I'm very mixed-up.

DIONYSUS. Yes.

PENTHEUS. Nervous.

DIONYSUS. Afraid; that's natural.

PENTHEUS. Yes. More than that, though. I've been finding out too much. Perhaps I shouldn't interfere. They'll return to the city. That's where they live. It's their business what they do here.

DIONYSUS. A sickness, you said. Don't you have responsibilities?

PENTHEUS. In matters of the mind, who knows what sickness is?

DIONYSUS. You do. Why else are you king? (*Pause.*) Come! I shall help Your Majesty to see clearly.

PENTHEUS. Well, I won't have *you* looking.

DIONYSUS. No, no. Everything now is reserved for you.

PENTHEUS. I've always behaved in a civilized manner.

DIONYSUS *takes* PENTHEUS' *bag and shoe.* PENTHEUS *climbs the tree. Lights fade at the foot of tree. At the top,* PENTHEUS *is lit.*

Lights come up on the WOMEN. *This scene was called 'Flower Unfolding' because that is how it should look at the beginning. The* WOMEN *are grouped round* AGAVE, *and are quite still. Then slowly the group begins to move: the* FOURTH *and* FIFTH WOMEN *roll outwards, and become fascinated with some physical object belonging to the* FIFTH WOMAN – *her hair, or something she wears: it has a special texture to them: touching it is for wonder. The* WOMAN SECRETARY *slowly stands. She stands rigidly against the tree, and begins a humming sound, all on one note.* AGAVE *holds her hand up in front of her and above her to examine it. The* FIRST WOMAN *assumes a foetal position. The* SECOND WOMAN *is unnaturally still, and when she does move (as under) it will be sudden. The* THIRD WOMAN *says, with discovery, 'Amersham'. At first it is the name of a town, then it becomes 'Am a sham' then 'Mama sham', then a stream of gibberish using only those syllables. When* DIONYSUS *steps over her, 'Sham' will be a short cry of pain (though he does not touch her) after which the gibberish fades out.*

AGAVE *looks up at her hand, and suddenly laughs.*

DIONYSUS strolls over from the bottom of the tree, to join the WOMEN. When he questions AGAVE, it will be as though the words took a while to travel through the air to reach her, so that there is always a beat before she answers.

DIONYSUS. What do you see?
AGAVE. Bones.

DIONYSUS puts his own hand in front of her.

DIONYSUS. And now?
AGAVE. Bones.

The SECOND WOMAN is the only one who feels a wish to talk, and she moves among the audience. She wishes to explain to them. She is very controlled in speech and movement, and it is not always clear that the audience she is addressing is the one actually present.

SECOND WOMAN. The expression 'to take a trip' refers, of course, to the interior voyage. This is the experience of which an acid-head will tell you that it has changed his life, and if he is honest, he will admit that the change may not always be for the better.
AGAVE. Hand bones.
DIONYSUS. Connected to the?
AGAVE. Wrist bone.
DIONYSUS. Connected to the?

AGAVE laughs.

SECOND WOMAN. The mushroom itself has the interesting side-effect that it confers –

She has reached a chair, the back of which has been weakened. She hits it with the side of her hand. It breaks.

– great strength. Though whether this is a real increase in physical strength, or only that one no longer notices pain, is a matter for dispute.

DIONYSUS *points up at* PENTHEUS.

DIONYSUS. And in the tree?
AGAVE (*looks*). Bones.

DIONYSUS. Connected to the?
AGAVE. Tree bone.

AGAVE *laughs. The* WOMAN SECRETARY *joins in.*

DIONYSUS. Man bones or monkey bones?
AGAVE. Bone bones.

DIONYSUS *moves quickly away from* AGAVE *to a position near the tree. He gives the call of a children's game.*

DIONYSUS. Olly-olly-oxen! Olly-olly-oxen! Olly-olly-ox an'
    free!

All the WOMEN *but* AGAVE *respond. They become like little girls, and run to* DIONYSUS, *who points up at the tree, reciting what sounds like a children's rhyme.*

DIONYSUS. Come and see
    The monkey in the tree.
FIRST WOMAN. Monkey got a flea.
FIFTH WOMAN. Monkey wants a pee.

They all giggle.

FOURTH WOMAN. He can't pee on me.
    He'll have to pee on thee.

More giggling and little girl silliness ad lib: 'You are *awful*;' 'Did you hear what she said?' 'She said, "pee": she used a word.' 'Monkey pee! Monkey pee!' *They take up the words as a song, and begin to dance around* DIONYSUS.

WOMEN. A B C.
    Monkey in the tree!
    He can't pee on me.
FOURTH WOMAN. He'll have to pee on the flea.

They think this is an even better joke than the last. But DIONYSUS *stoops, picks up an imaginary stone, and plays with it, throwing it up and catching it. They stop giggling, and watch him. Suddenly he throws it viciously at* PENTHEUS.
    PENTHEUS *gives a cry.*
    Silence.

FOURTH WOMAN (*hesitantly*). A . . . B . . . C . . . (*Stops.*)

DIONYSUS. A B C.
  The monkey's in the tree.
  Who'll knock the monkey
  Out of the tree?
AGAVE. Bones.
THIRD WOMAN. Girls can't throw, actually. Everybody knows
  that.
DIONYSUS. Try.

He gives her an imaginary stone, and guides her arm as she throws. PENTHEUS *almost falls from the tree, trying to get out of the way. He is frightened.*

  Who'll knock the monkey
  Out of the tree?

Ad libs as all but AGAVE *scramble for imaginary stones, and throw* – 'I hit him.' 'You didn't.' 'Monkey! Monkey!' AGAVE *remains apart, but she repeats,* 'Knock down the bones! Knock down the bones!'

PENTHEUS (*shouts*). Stop it!

Silence.

  I'm coming down.

Pause. Then he descends.

FOURTH WOMAN. Monkey made a noise.
FIRST WOMAN. Monkey made words?
DIONYSUS. That's a talking monkey.

PENTHEUS *has reached ground level.*

PENTHEUS. I am not a monkey.

Pause. They surround him.

DIONYSUS. If he's not a monkey, what is he?
PENTHEUS. You know very well who I am.
AGAVE. Bones.
DIONYSUS. Is he a frog? He's a frog.
SECOND WOMAN. Jump, frog.

She is standing behind him, gives him a pinch, and he jumps. They laugh.

FOURTH WOMAN. He's a frog.

DIONYSUS. Is he a snake? He's a snake.

The SECOND WOMAN *pushes* PENTHEUS *so that he falls to the ground.*

SECOND WOMAN. Slither, snake!

They laugh.

THIRD WOMAN. *That's* not a snake.

PENTHEUS *gets up as far as all fours.*

PENTHEUS. Please stand out of the way. I wish to leave.

DIONYSUS. Is he a cuddly fawn? Yes, he's a cuddly fawn.

SECOND WOMAN (*advances*). Cummere, fawn. I'm going to cuddle you.

At once the WOMEN *become competitive cuddlers, all trying to cuddle the fawn at once.* 'Let me cuddle the fawn.' 'I want the fawn.' 'He's mine.' 'Come on, Bambi,' 'I'm going to cuddle him.' PENTHEUS *manages to burst out of the ring of them, but falls back again.*

PENTHEUS (*as he does so*). Take your hands off me!

Silence. They recoil.

DIONYSUS. That's a *dangerous* animal.

PENTHEUS. Be quiet. You've said enough.

DIONYSUS. Listen to him snarl. (*Snarling noise.*)

FIRST WOMAN (*not quite convinced*). He's snarling?

DIONYSUS. Growling.

FIFTH WOMAN. He's angry, isn't he?

DIONYSUS. Better be careful. Keep away.

PENTHEUS (*to the* FIRST WOMAN). Please help me up.

DIONYSUS. Keep away. He's a killer.

PENTHEUS. I've hurt my foot.

DIONYSUS. He wants to kill you. He's crouched to spring.

SECOND WOMAN. Wicked!

THIRD WOMAN. Vicious!

PENTHEUS. Ladies, you can see that I am unarmed –

DIONYSUS. A real killer!

PENTHEUS. – and at your mercy.

DIONYSUS. A very dangerous animal!

AGAVE. What animal?

DIONYSUS *goes quickly to her.*

DIONYSUS. Down there. In front of the women.

AGAVE. I see ... bones.

DIONYSUS. Crouching bones.

AGAVE. Yes.

PENTHEUS (*to the* WOMEN). First, the heel came off my shoe.
I've had difficulty in walking. Something went, I think,
when you pushed me over. It's only a sprain. It's really not
serious.

DIONYSUS (*to* AGAVE). A puma. A mountain lion.

AGAVE *looks at her own hand.*

AGAVE. Bones. And the veins knotted like string. No flesh.
I see beneath the surface of things. Below the appearance.
That's wisdom, I suppose. I did not see the veins at first,
but if I concentrate I can see them.

DIONYSUS *takes her hand, and brings it down so that it points
to* PENTHEUS.

DIONYSUS. Connected to the?

She begins to move, taking a circling path, to get a better look at
PENTHEUS.

PENTHEUS. What are you doing? What are you doing?

AGAVE (*looking at* PENTHEUS). Muscles? Sinews?

DIONYSUS. And in the mouth?

Pause.

AGAVE. Teeth.

PENTHEUS. What are you doing?

DIONYSUS. A mountain lion! They're waiting for you. You
are the leader.

Slowly AGAVE *takes her place in front of the* WOMEN.

PENTHEUS. Mother?

DIONYSUS *repeats* 'Mother', *but uses the* 'er' *of the word to
make a growling sound that ends in a roar.*

AGAVE. What? ... What? ...

PENTHEUS *begins to crawl towards her. The* WOMEN *are*

F

frightened, and back away, crying 'Ma'am!' *in various accents of dismay. Only* AGAVE *does not move.*

AGAVE (*to the* WOMEN, *soothing*). It's all right . . . It's all right.

PENTHEUS *reaches her. He puts out an arm to her. She backs a step away. Terrified cries from the* WOMEN.
  PENTHEUS *crawls nearer. He pulls off his wig.*

PENTHEUS. Mother, –

DIONYSUS *takes up the* 'er' *to roar.*

  It's I –

DIONYSUS *uses the* 'I'.

  Your son.

DIONYSUS *uses the* 'your', *repeating it as two roars.*

  PENTHEUS *reaches out again to pull himself up. As he touches her,* AGAVE *lashes out with the side of her hand, as we have seen the* SECOND WOMAN *do earlier.* PENTHEUS *gives a cry. He is thrown back some distance, and his arm seems to be broken.*
  AGAVE *laughs.*
  PENTHEUS *begins to whimper.*

AGAVE. Bones . . . break.

She comes towards him slowly. PENTHEUS *is frightened and tries to move away. She is flexing her hands. Only* PENTHEUS *and* AGAVE *are lit.*

PENTHEUS. No, mother. No, mother. No. No.
AGAVE (*gentle*). Oh, yes . . . Yes.

He already has one hand up, trying feebly to keep her away. She pulls up his broken arm so that now both arms are stretched towards her, and as she clasps him, the two – mother and son – are embracing. He whimpers with pain as she does this. Then she kisses him, and her arms tighten. He gives a long scream as the lights fade.
  Black Out. But no silence. PENTHEUS' *scream is taken up; – as if it had travelled across the stage. Now it is the* JUNIOR SECRETARY *who is screaming. He is on the middle platform with the* PRINCIPAL PRIVATE SECRETARY *and the* SENIOR SECRE-

TARY, *the* PRINCIPAL PRIVATE SECRETARY *supporting him,*
as he screams and screams.

Under cover of the noise and darkness, PENTHEUS, DIONYSUS
AGAVE *and the* WOMEN *clear. A five-second black-out should be*
enough.

Lights up to show who is screaming. Then the JUNIOR SECRE-
TARY *recovers, and continues his story.*

JUNIOR SECRETARY. She was possessed, crazed, possessed
    totally.
  She did not hear his cries.
  Instead she seized his wounded arm,
  Braced her foot upon his chest, and pulled. She pulled
    away
  The arm from its shoulder socket. This was not her
    strength.
  It was some god's strength coursing within a woman's arm.
  So much for the king's mother. At his other side
  Ringed hands scratched off his flesh, and the whole pack,
  Was rending him. He screamed for a little while,
  Though the noise they made came near to drowning his.
  One tore off an arm, another a foot –
  A foot in silk, wearing a heel-less shoe.
  His ribs were stripped clean of flesh, and every arm
  Was red, as they flung his flesh from hand to hand,
  Playing ball with bits of his body.
  What was left when they had finished
  Lies in the forest, strewn among the rocks,
  Hanging from the branches of trees,
  Lost, anonymous, waiting to be reclaimed.
  His mother has his head.
  She thinks it is the head of a mountain lion she has caught.
  She carries it in triumph, and will bring it here.
  She will show you her trophy, and demand your admiration.
  But all her triumph
  Is only the promise of grief.
        Before she returns, I will leave you.
  I have seen too much sorrow to bear more here.

A wise man will not meddle with the gods,
But pay his dues – reverence, humility,
And above all, self-effacement.

As he leaves, martial music is heard. He hurries away. AGAVE
*her hands, face and blouse stained with blood, marches in with the
almost equally bloodstained* WOMEN. AGAVE *is carrying* PEN-
THEUS' *bloody head. She will use, in her commands, the non-
sensical military pronunciation that makes* 'Left! Right!' *into*
'Hep! Ha!', 'Halt!' *into a glottal* 'Hoh!' *and* 'Ease' *into* 'Ice'.

AGAVE. Left, right! Left, right! Left, right!
　　Squad, halt!
　　Left turn! (*Or right depending on how the director has chosen
　　　to bring them in.*)
　　Stand at ease!
　　Stand easy!

She turns towards the PRINCIPAL PRIVATE SECRETARY *and*
SENIOR SECRETARY.

　　Gentlemen,
　　The women of the city have returned from hunting.
　　We expect your welcome and your congratulations.

The PRINCIPAL PRIVATE SECRETARY *looks for help to the*
SENIOR SECRETARY, *and does not get it.*

PPS. Welcome.
AGAVE. We bring this trophy to the palace.
　　We have had happy hunting, a successful day.
　　Look! Look at the prize I bring –
　　A mountain lion, caught and killed by women,
　　By unarmed women, hunting on Mount Cythaeron.
PPS. Who killed him?
AGAVE. I. I struck him first.
　　I, Agave, the Queen.
PPS. And then?
FIRST WOMAN. I.
WOMAN SECRETARY. I.
THIRD WOMAN. I.
FOURTH WOMAN. I.

FIFTH WOMAN. I.

SECOND WOMAN. All struck him. All killed.

AGAVE. But after me. I was the first to reach him.
You see the result.

PPS. Yes. I see it.

AGAVE. All may share my glory. All women.
All may share the glory –

She licks blood from her hand.

– and the feast.

See!

She lifts the head.

This lion cub is young and proud.
Beneath the soft mane, its cheeks are smooth.
A young lion, a king.
But the god we serve is more cunning than kings,
And knows the ways of beasts.
He found the prey, and set the dancing women
On to catch a lion.

SECOND WOMAN. We follow a great hunter.

AGAVE. And deserve some praise, I think.
It has been a poor reception so far.

The SENIOR SECRETARY *rises, and comes to the front of the platform.*

SENIOR SECRETARY. I praise you.
And Pentheus, your son?

AGAVE. Will praise his mother, who with naked hands,
Killed a great quarry, a mountain lion.

SENIOR SECRETARY. You are proud of this action, clearly.

AGAVE. Proud and happy.
I have brought back a great trophy, as any man may see.

SENIOR SECRETARY. Then show the citizens of Thebes
This trophy of yours. This head
You have brought from the hunt.
Show them all.

AGAVE *shows off the head to the audience.*

AGAVE. You citizens of our orderly city,
  People of Thebes, look what I have brought.
  Here is the noble head of a noble beast.
  We did not use nets, or bows and arrows, spears or guns.
  Our hands were enough, our own white hands,
  The delicate hands of women.
  Where are the men who boast of their hunting,
  And carry an armoury with them into the forest?
  With our bare hands we hunted this beast,
  Caught it, and cornered it, and tore it to pieces.
    Now where is my son, Pentheus the king?
  I will have him set this head on a wall in the palace,
  This wild lion I have caught and killed.
  He shall place it first among those his father brought from
    the hunt.
  Among all those heads, this shall have pride of place.

The POLICEMAN *enters, followed by two* ATTENDANTS, *bearing
the body of* PENTHEUS *in a box, which is covered by a cloth,
discoloured with blood.*

POLICEMAN. Follow me!
  You carry a dead weight, I know. Set it down there
  In front of the palace. Sirs, this was Pentheus,
  Whose body after a long search
  I have gathered together from Cythaeron's slopes,
  Where it lay dismembered, scattered in pieces, shreds,
  No two pieces lying side by side.
  There, as I searched among the pines and larches,
  I found some of the women who had done this murder,
  Still deep in the lethargy that follows madness.
  But most, they said, had gone on with Agave,
  Back to the city. And what they said, I see, is true.
AGAVE. Fetch my son. Fetch my son here.
  Call him to look upon his mother's triumph.
  For I have left the triviality of daily things.
  I have been hunting animals with my bare hands,
  With these hands that hold the trophy I have won.
  Why will you not glory in it, and share my triumph?

PPS. This is a grief so great, it cannot be defined.
  I cannot look.
  Majesty, you have done a murder, and now you invite
  The city to share in your act.
  How terribly I pity you, and all of us.
  The god who is in our blood has punished this city.
  We would not worship him, and he left us leaderless.
  We have no head now.
  The mind which governed our city and kept our laws
  Has been destroyed.
AGAVE. How grumpy and grudging you are, old before your
    time.
  I hope my son has enough of his mother in him
  To find enjoyment in another's happiness.
  Call him out. Someone call him out.
  Let him see me here triumphant before you all.
PPS. No more, lady. No more.
  When you realize what you have done,
  You will suffer beyond reckoning. Only if the gods are
    merciful,
  Your present madness may last until you die.
  Then you will think yourself happy, and thinking so, be so.
AGAVE. Why do you reproach me? Is something wrong?
  Have I done wrong?
PPS (*to the* SENIOR SECRETARY). We must take her inside.
  Enough has been said here.
SENIOR SECRETARY. No.
PPS. What?
SENIOR SECRETARY. Let her see, since we do.
  (*To* AGAVE.) Majesty, look up at the sky.
AGAVE (*looking*). At the sky? Why?
SENIOR SECRETARY. What do you see there?
AGAVE. I see sky. What else is there to see?
SENIOR SECRETARY. Does it look as it always looks?
AGAVE. How should I know how it always looks?
  It looks as it looks.
  I know it is sky, and I see sky,
  Through it and to it.

SENIOR SECRETARY. An excellent description. Look down
    now slowly.
    Look at my hand.

He is holding out his hand for her to see.

    And what do you see?
AGAVE. Bones.
SENIOR SECRETARY. Ah! Is that it?
    But you know it is a hand!
AGAVE. Of course.
    A hand is a hand.
SENIOR SECRETARY. Of bones?
AGAVE. Yes.
SENIOR SECRETARY. But of something else. There is more
    to a hand.
    Look closely. Concentrate.
PPS. No more.
SENIOR SECRETARY. Oh much more. We have hardly
    started.
AGAVE. I see the blood, moving through vein and artery.
    I see muscle and cartilage.
SENIOR SECRETARY. Good. Very good.
    'Muscle and cartilage' is good. (*Takes his hand away
    quickly.*)
    Do you remember what was said to you
    A moment ago?

Pause. AGAVE *discovers she can't remember.*

AGAVE. No, I have forgotten. We were speaking . . .
    We were speaking of hunting.
SENIOR SECRETARY (*shows her his hand again*). It doesn't
    matter.
    Concentrate on my hand. Do you see the outline now?
AGAVE. Outline?
SENIOR SECRETARY. The skin stretched over the flesh
    That covers the bone.
    It is like that with hands:
    Bone and muscle and vein
    Are covered with flesh and fat, and the flesh with skin.

Nails at the ends of the fingers, (*Showing the back.*)
Some dirt beneath the nails.
There are lines on the palm of my hand; (*Showing the front.*)
A life line, a love line, Majesty,
My fate and my character, do you see, in my palm?
Concentrate.
Do you see the lines of my life in the palm of my hand?

Pause.

AGAVE. I see your hand, skin and bones and the rest.
Your life line is not greatly important to me.
SENIOR SECRETARY. And what are you carrying, Majesty,
Between your own hands?
PPS. That's enough.
SENIOR SECRETARY. What are you carrying there?

AGAVE *is frightened, and will not look.*

AGAVE. A lion's head. We caught a lion on the mountain.

She turns to the WOMEN *for corroboration.*

We caught a young lion on the mountain. You remember
that.
Somebody tell him I have a lion's head in my hands.
SENIOR SECRETARY. Look directly at it.
AGAVE (*to* WOMEN). Tell him what I am holding in my hands.
SENIOR SECRETARY. Just look. Look closely.
Take all the time you need.

AGAVE *looks. Silence.*
AGAVE *gives a long cry.*

Is it a lion's head still?
AGAVE. No! No! Oh, no, no!
I see a grief I hold in my hands.
I see the greatest grief a mother knows
Between my hands. It is my son's head.
(*To the* WOMEN.) Who killed my son? (*No response.*)
Speak! Why don't you speak?
My heart is breaking, and you keep silent.

SENIOR SECRETARY. You killed him, Majesty, you and
  your women.
  You killed him on the mountain.
AGAVE (*doesn't understand*). What?
  Why should he go to the mountain?
PPS. To see what you were doing. Exactly.
AGAVE. No more than that?
PPS. Something more than that.

AGAVE *turns to the box containing the body.*

AGAVE. To destroy everything like Bluebeard's wife for
  curiosity?
  To change our pride to sorrow and disgrace?
  Upon these hands with which once I nursed him,
  There is now his blood. These are the hands
  With which I waved to the cheering people.
  White hands in a gilt coach, waving to the people,
  Now bloody and disgraced.
  How with these guilty hands may I touch his body?
  How can I, cursed with his blood, prepare him for burial?
PPS. It is not proper.
AGAVE. And who else will do it?

She nurses the head as if it were a baby.

  No, child. No hands can give you proper care
  Unless my own hands undo my own work.

*She takes off her own bloodstained scarf as a wrapping for the
head.*

  Dearest face of my dead son!
  Soft lips that I remember at my breast!
  Now with this scarf, I wrap your head,

*She pulls back the covering from the box to lay the head inside,
and almost faints at what she sees.*

  Laying it, –

She forces herself to continue.

  Laying it with the mangled flesh that was once my flesh,
  That lived within me before I gave it birth.

PPS. He denied the god. So did we all.
   And we have all been punished.
AGAVE (*to the body*). You were my only son.
   The city looked up to you. You guarded and guided us,
   Keeping us from discontent.
   Here in Thebes, you ran an orderly city.
   Now it is all gone, all that order gone,
   And what shall follow it is not easily known.
   I must go. I must leave the city.
   I have killed my son. There is no place for me here.
   What would you have said if you had lived,
   'Diminished responsibility'? You would have said,
            'We don't hang people in Thebes.'
   What would you have done with me? –
   A woman mad with drugs who killed her son.

Thunder. Lights change.

   DIONYSUS *appears on the upper platform. Instead of the beat
clothes he has worn before, he is now seen in a fawnskin with
buskins and he wears gilded horns. All kneel except* AGAVE,
the PRINCIPAL PRIVATE SECRETARY *and the* SENIOR
SECRETARY.

DIONYSUS. I am Dionysus, born of no human father,
   The son of Zeus himself.
   Here in Thebes I have been blasphemed.
   Here you have denied me, and you see my revenge.
   Your King has found the death which he deserved.
   He has been torn to pieces by what he most denied:
   Denied because he feared it, knew it within himself,
   Went out to meet it even when he denied it.
   Mother and son are one flesh.
   His own flesh killed him.
   This was the old justice, the justice which is not wisdom,
      not considered, not fair,
   The justice of custom, of what is known and has always
      been done,
   The final justice of blood.
   By that same justice,

You, Agave, shall be driven out to wander in misery and pain.
What you have done, you have done at my will.
You have been my instrument, no more than that.
Yet you are unclean.
You have killed your son, and must suffer for it.
PPS. Be merciful, Dionysus. We know we have been wrong.
DIONYSUS. Too late. When there was time, you still denied
 me.
PPS. But we have learned. We have all learned.
 Your sentence is disproportionate to the offence.
DIONYSUS. I am a god. You blasphemed me.
PPS. Gods should be free from human passions.
DIONYSUS. What god are you to tell a god how to behave?

Light dies on him.

AGAVE. Well, that is my sentence, then. I shall not regret it.
 (*To* ATTENDANTS.) Take up the body, and follow. I owe
 a burial.
To these pieces of my son.
I am to be a traveller now, far from Cythaeron.
There will be no hunting for me, and no dancing,
Neither old ways, nor new ways.
Only my own lonely ways to go.
(*To the* WOMEN.) So may you find another lady to lead you,
Another city to bring to the worship of Dionysus,
Another mother to kill her son.
(*To the* PRINCIPAL PRIVATE SECRETARY.) And fare you
 well.
PPS. Farewell to you, unhappy majesty.
 Farewell. Though you may find it weary faring.

She begins to go. Then turns back.
 Lights fade until only she is lit.

AGAVE. Why? Why?
PPS. He was trying to understand you.
SENIOR SECRETARY. He was trying to understand you.
AGAVE. Oh, was that it?

Fade to Black.

Methuen's Modern Plays

Edited by John Cullen

Methuen's Theatre Classics

Methuen Playscripts

John McGrath	EVENTS WHILE GUARDING THE BOFORS GUN
David Mercer	THE GOVERNOR'S LADY
Georges Michel	THE SUNDAY WALK
Rodney Milgate	A REFINED LOOK AT EXISTENCE
Guillaume Oyono-Mbia	THREE SUITORS: ONE HUSBAND and UNTIL FURTHER NOTICE
Alan Plater	CLOSE THE COALHOUSE DOOR
David Selbourne	THE PLAY OF WILLIAM COOPER AND EDMUND DEW-NEVETT
Johnny Speight	IF THERE WEREN'T ANY BLACKS YOU'D HAVE TO INVENT THEM
Martin Sperr	TALES FROM LANDSHUT
Lanford Wilson	HOME FREE! and THE MADNESS OF LADY BRIGHT

Other Plays from Methuen

Jean Anouilh	COLLECTED PLAYS, VOLUME I (The Ermine, Thieves' Carnival, Restless Heart, Traveller Without Luggage, Dinner with the Family)
	COLLECTED PLAYS, VOLUME II (Time Remembered, Point of Departure, Antigone, Romeo and Jeanette, Medea)
Jean Giraudoux	PLAYS, VOLUME I (Tiger at the Gates, Duel of Angels, Judith)
	PLAYS, VOLUME II (Amphitryon, Intermezzo, Ondine)
John Millington Synge	PLAYS AND POEMS

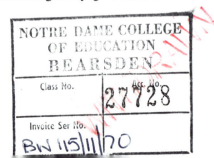